CROMFORD &
HIGH PEAK

By
I.C.Coleford

Middleton Top PHOTOGRAPH: N. Stead Collection

IRWELL
PRESS

Copyright Irwell Press
ISBN 1-871608-78-3

Acknowledgements

This book, although a modest little offering, is the result of considerable primary source research. Among the documents studied are the Cromford & High Peak Railway minute books and correspondence books, London & North Western Railway Locomotive Committee minutes, various Board of Trade reports and railway company Working Time Tables (WTTs), most of which were examined at the Public Record Office, Kew. For reference, the relevant files include: RAIL144/1, 144/2, 144/5 and 144/6 (C&HPR documents); RAIL410 series (LNWR minutes); RAIL912/133 (WTTs); RAIL1053/123 (accident report); MT6 1/192 and 1/199 (Board of Trade files).

Secondary sources include *The Cromford & High Peak Railway* by A.Rimmer (Oakwood Press 1985), and various issues of the *Railway Observer*, the *SLS Journal, Railway Magazine*, and *Railway and Travel Monthly.*

Last, but certainly not least, sincere thanks are due to Messrs. Allan Brackenbury and Justin McCarthy (of the Railway & Canal Historical Society), Bryan Wilson, Alan Rimmer, John Ryan, Paul Gilson and Obediah Slope for their invaluable assistance with this project.

Photograph front cover: During the C&HPR's later years, in particular, its unsuitability for large, modern mineral wagons was a significant handicap – see page 23. PHOTOGRAPH: Derek Cross
Photograph rear cover: The incline at Sheep Pasture, looking east in March 1966. PHOTOGRAPH: Andrew Muckley.

First Published in the United Kingdom by
IRWELL PRESS 1996
59A High Street, Clophill, Bedfordshire MK45 4BE
Printed and Bound by Irwell Press, Enfield, London

Contents

Top of the incline at Sheep Pasture, March 1966. PHOTOGRAPH: Andrew Muckley

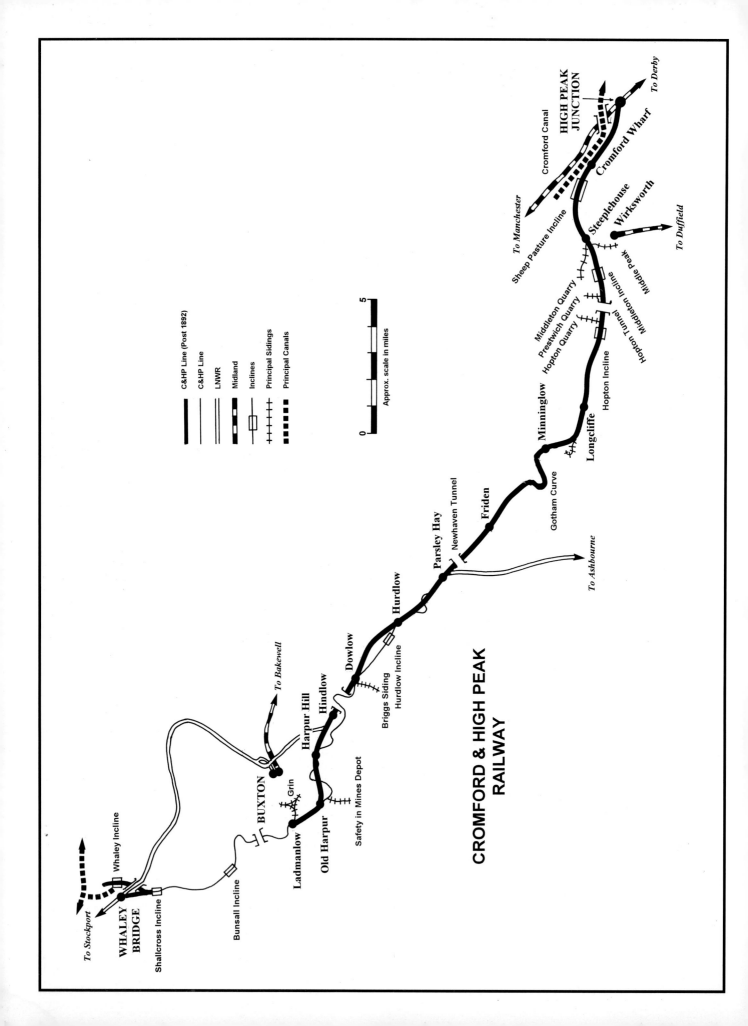

CROMFORD & HIGH PEAK RAILWAY

1....Mainly Historical

Among the many aspects of the C&HPR's mystique was its scenic appeal, traversing, for much of its length, magnificently bleak, uninhabited terrain. That aspect is ably illustrated here - J94 No.68012, one water tank and a brake van cross the embankment, a little over the 1,000ft contour, just to the east of Minninglow on 12 July 1966. PHOTOGRAPH: IVO PETERS

'If the character of the C&HPR line were to be made first class so as to run through trains at high speeds, it would become a competitor to the LNWR.....'

The Cromford & High Peak Railway (C&HPR) was one of the most distinctive railways in the country. It had various claims to fame, among them its rope worked inclines - latterly two, but originally nine - and also a 1 in 14 incline which, for a period of ninety years, was routinely worked by adhesion. The railway's mystique was boosted by its 'out-of-the-way' nature - much of the route was over 1,000ft up on the Derbyshire hills amid exquisite but rugged terrain, and from 1954 onwards the nearest passenger station was some 1^1/2 miles away. Right until the end of its operational life in 1967, the C&HPR showed evidence of its origins - those origins had their roots in the mid-1820s, at the very beginning of the transition from the canal and tramway era to the railway age. So - why was a railway built at such a comparatively early date across such bleak terrain?

Background

The C&HPR was conceived primarily as a connection between the Cromford Canal, a little to the south of Matlock, and the Peak Forest Canal at Whaley Bridge. The Cromford Canal had opened in 1792 (also quoted as 1794) and the Peak Forest Canal in 1800, but the two waterways were separated by the seemingly impenetrable massif of Derbyshire's Peak District. The usefulness of joining the two canals, thus providing a link between the East Midlands and the rapidly growing manufacturing towns of South Lancashire, prompted thoughts of a connecting canal across the hills, and in 1810 the eminent engineer, Sir John Rennie, surveyed a possible route. However, Rennie's proposal was not acted upon. This was due to two main factors - firstly, the estimated cost was £650,000 and, secondly, there was the problem of keeping water in a canal which, for a distance of 20-odd miles, would cross nothing but limestone.

In 1824 a committee was appointed to carry the embryo C&HPR into effect, and at a meeting held on 16 June of that year it was resolved that subscriptions be invited. The target was £50,000 in £100 shares. Less than six weeks later - on 28 July - it was reported that the whole of the share issue had been subscribed. The railway's attraction was not only as a means of connection between the Cromford and the High Peak Canals. It was also expected to lure through traffic between the East Midlands and South Lancashire while, more locally, it was anticipated that the railway would promote the development of quarries in its catchment area. In the railway company's formative period a branch line to Macclesfield was considered, but that proposal was abandoned at an early stage.

The next step was for a route to be surveyed. This task was undertaken by Josias Jessop, whose favoured route was, in fact, similar to that of Rennie's proposed canal of 1810. Jessop reported back to the railway committee on 1 September 1824. Apart from his observations about the proposed route (more of which anon), he cal-

culated, most encouragingly, that the line would probably generate well over £18,000-worth of traffic per annum, calculated thus:In his report, Jessop explained that the population of Lancashire in 1821 was 1,052,859.....'and must have increased considerably since that period, from the immense increase of manufactures and trades, and may now be estimated at 1,200,000.....'. He stated that such a population was equivalent to more than one person per acre of land whereas the average for England was one person per three acres, and concluded that '.....the subsistence of two-thirds of Lancashire must be drawn from other sources'. On that basis, Jessop calculated that Lancashire had to 'import' some 400,000 tons of grain annually, and estimated that one tenth of that amount could be conveyed by the C&HPR (as listed in his estimate of traffic, over).

As for locally generated traffic, Jessop stated that the coals taken from Cromford exceeded 40,000 tons annually '.....and will of course increase with the greater facility of conveyance'. (His estimate, above, was based on 60,000 tons being conveyed by the railway annually). And there was stone: '.....the Hopton Wood stone has hitherto been limited in its sale only by the means of conveying it away, and will become an extensive article of carriage. The large flat Paving Stone, which is of excellent quality, and Stone Slates produced at Goyt's Clough Quarries, the Lime-Stone, Grit-Stone, Minerals etc. will be very considerable....'

Let it not be forgotten that all this was taking place in 1824. To put things into perspective, that was a year before the famous Stockton &

Grain - 40,000 tons carried 30 miles at 2d per ton per mile:	£10,000
Coal - 60,000 tons, on the average carried 10 miles at 1d:	£ 2,500
Lime and limestone - 10,000 tons carried 8 miles at 1d:	£333
Paving stones, slate etc. - 10,000 tons carried 30 miles at 1d:	£1,250
Hopton Wood Stone and Gritstone - 5,000 tons, 20m. at 1d	£468
Pig Iron, Bar Iron and Lead - 4,000 tons, 30 miles at 1d:	£500
Timber, Hay etc. - 1,000 tons, 30 miles at 1d:	£125
Wool and Cotton (raw) - 2,000 tons, 30 miles at 2d:	£500
Nottingham, Derby and Leicester Trade to Manchester and the Neighbourhood - 2,000 tons, 30 miles at 2d:	£500
Manchester Trade to the Southward and Eastward - 5,000 tons, 30 miles at 2d:	£1,250
Huddersfield and Yorkshire Trade - 1,000 tons, 30 miles at 2d:	£250
Groceries, Spirits etc. - 1,000 tons, 30 miles at 2d:	£250
Sundries as Hops, Cheese, Salt, Earthenware, Dying and Bleaching Goods, Moulding Sand, Provisions, and many other Articles - 3,000tn, 30m. at 2d:	£750

Darlington Railway was opened, and six years before Britain's first major passenger-carrying 'main' line, the Liverpool & Manchester Railway, was unveiled. The C&HPR - 33 miles of public railway - was a truly pioneering venture, especially as the initial plans included the possible use of locomotives. It is, therefore, understandable that, despite its seemingly modest status as a goods-only link between two canals, the railway generated such interest and support. Another perceived 'miracle' of the railway scheme was that the estimated cost of constructing the line - £149,206.16s.8d - was less than a quarter of the projected cost of Rennie's canal scheme of 1810. That estimate was for a standard gauge railway built to the alignment detailed in Jessop's survey of August/September 1824, save for one significant revision. The original survey had favoured a 1,400-yard tunnel through limestone near 'Haven Lodge' (a little to the south of Parsley Hay), but the revised route avoided the necessity for a tunnel by means of '....an ascent of an eleventh of an inch in a yard after passing the Embankment near Pike Hall, and continuing that ascent for 3¹/₂ miles, which leaves a deep cutting of 24 feet at the brow of the hill'.

Jessop explained that: 'The Railway is proposed to be constructed on the system of Levels and Inclined Planes, by which Steam Engines may be employed as the moving power to convey the Waggons. The locomotive or travelling Engines being used on the Level Parts, and stationary Engines at the Inclined Planes. Railways so constructed are equally adapted to the employment of Engines or Horses, for on the level parts, the friction of the Wheels of the Locomotive Carriages against the Rails is sufficient to propel them. As Steam Engines, where the trade is extensive, have many advantages over Horses, conveying at much less cost and with greater expedition, it would be desirable for the Committee to obtain powers, to enable the Company of Proprietors, either to become the Carriers, or agree with Individuals, who may be disposed to embark capital in the Waggons and Engines for that purpose; this is the more necessary, as from the greater velocity with which Steam Engines may travel, Horses and Engines could not use the Railway in common without disadvantage'. Jessop went to considerable lengths to exhort the advantages of locomotive traction, but as we shall see later, the C&HPR was initially worked by horses.

When it came to raising the £150,000 to construct the railway and equip it with 'steam engines' (stationary engines and/or locomotives), £70,000 had, in fact, already been subscribed '....by the Noblemen, Gentlemen and Landowners in the immediate neighbourhood....'. The balance was taken up so quickly that six subscriptions, amounting to no less than £33,500, had to be excluded. (The company's total capital was subsequently revised at £164,000). With the preliminaries completed, the next stage was to secure the requisite Act of Parliament, and this was obtained on 2 May 1825. Then came the construction......

It took five years before the first section of the C&HPR was completed, the Cromford Wharf-Hurdlow section (16 miles) opening on 29 May 1830. The Hurdlow-Whaley Bridge section 16³/₄ miles), which completed the line, did not open until 6 July 1831.

The Inclines

As already explained, the C&HPR was not a continuous stretch of conventional railway. Far from it. It was punctuated by no less than nine steeply graded inclines, and wagons had to be brought up and down each incline on chains, the movement of which was controlled by stationary winding engines. Although this was considered somewhat innovative in 1820s Derbyshire, the practice was by no means unique - it had first been seen at Birtley Fell in County Durham in 1808, and had subsequently found widespread favour, particularly on the colliery lines in the North-east of England.

On the C&HPR, during the nineteenth century, several of the inclines were abandoned, circumvented, merged or, in one case, given over to locomotive working, leaving only three operational in the present century. However, they were such a famous feature of the line that it is appropriate to deal with them at this early juncture.

The principle of chain working on inclines was actually quite simple. Wagons were attached to a continuous chain, the chain being fastened to the last wagon of ascending trains and the first wagon of descending ones. The chain passed around two pulleys - the pulley at the top of the incline was in the engine house and was driven by the winding engine, while the pulley at the bottom was situated in a pit beneath the tracks. The weight of ascending wagons was counterbalanced by descending ones (descending loads being heavier), and so the winding engine needed only to control the speed of the run, rather than physically haul the wagons. Consequently, the engines did not have to possess gargantuan power. The balancing of loads on the C&HPR was calculated on the basis of one loaded or three empty wagons ascending being equivalent to two loaded or five empties descending.

Because of the inclines, wagons with less than 10 inches clearance above rail level were prohibited, as they would not pass over the sheaves of the rope apparatus. In later years, when only Sheep Pasture and Middleton Inclines remained operational, such wagons were officially banned between Longcliffe and Cromford Junction. Another requirement was that wagons with end doors had to be taken up and down the inclines with doors uppermost, and for this purpose a turning triangle was provided between Dowlow and Hindlow.

As for the C&HPR's haulage chains, they were originally supplied by Messrs. Pritt & Co. of Liverpool, but there were several instances of chains breaking - with potentially disastrous results - and although the blame could not be wholly placed on the manufacturer, the C&HPR sought guidance as to possible alternatives. In January 1836 the company looked to '.....ascertain comparative cost, weight and availability of ropes and chains', and requested an opinion '.....from the Liverpool & Manchester Railway as to how long a rope lasts on the inclined plane through the tunnel at the Liverpool end before a new one becomes necessary.....'. (It seems that that request had been prompted by a runaway at Whaley Incline which, at that time was worked by horses).

Whatever lessons were learned, in January 1836 the C&HPR invited the Coalbrookdale Iron Co. of Shifnal to submit quotes for chains of varying thickness' and, alternatively, for the supply of chain iron, from which chains could be made in the railway company's workshops at Cromford. Simultaneously, quotes were invited from Messrs. W.E.Slater of Eastwood for ropes of 3in., 4in., 6in., 9in. and 10in. thickness, white and tarred, but it is unclear whether such ropes were under realistic consideration for use on the inclines. The Coalbrookdale company won the day, and for the next nine years supplied chain iron to the C&HPR. In 1845 the C&HPR turned to the Butterley Iron Co. to supply its chain iron, while in 1849 the first of several orders was placed with Messrs. John & Charles Mold of the Alderwasley & Morley Park Iron Works near Derby. Mold's also took old chains in 'part exchange', presumably for their scrap value. Another supplier of chain iron surfaced in 1851 - this was the Codnor Park Ironworks, but dealings were not to the railway company's satisfaction, as evidenced by a letter from the C&HPR to Mr.Peter Bown on 17 October 1851: '.....the iron you sent is quite unfit for chain making.... we should like to return the remainder'.

By the mid-1850s there had been significant technical advances in the production of hemp ropes. At that time, the C&HPR was planning various improvements to the line, and it was decided that the use of hemp ropes instead of chains on the inclines would effect such a weight saving that, in two cases, pairs of adjacent inclines could be combined and worked as one. This brought about a very useful saving in journey times. Before long, though, the hemp ropes proved to be uncomfortably prone to breakages and so, from 1862, wire ropes were substituted. By 1868, all but one of the C&HPR's inclines had been equipped with new wire ropes. (The exception was Whaley Incline, which continued to use chains until the time of its closure in 1952).

As for the stationary engines, all nine on the C&HPR were supplied by the Butterley Iron Company, near Alfreton. The Butterley company provided an 'after sales' service to the C&HPR for many years, supplying spare parts and, occasionally, expertise. However, it would seem that the

The C&HPR incorporated a series of rope-worked inclined planes. This is Cromford Incline which, in 1857, was combined with Sheep Pasture Incline and worked as one continuous 1,320-yard plane. The grassy area between the curved section of track conceals an underground runaway pit, into which runaway wagons were diverted by means of catchpoints (these are discernible at the upper end of the pit). Alongside the catchpoints is the pointsman's cabin - the points were actually set for the pit, and if no warning of a runaway was received, the pointsman had to re-set the points for the 'main' line. The date is 22 July 1964, and the quiet stretch of road on the right of the picture is the main A6 trunk road. PHOTOGRAPH: PETER WARD

C&HPR did *not* use the Butterley company exclusively - the C&HPR's correspondence books contain a letter dated 31 May 1849 to Messrs. Peach & Sons, iron founders of Derby, requesting '.....two pistons for 20 horse engines - for which you have the pattern.....' .

The individual inclines and winding engines will be discussed in slightly greater detail elsewhere in this book.

For Better, For Worse....

Although the C&HPR had various claims to fame it was, in effect, actually little more than a tramroad company. It owned the entire line between Cromford and Whaley Bridge, but it did not work any of the traffic. Much of the traffic was worked by the local traders themselves - using their own horses and their own wagons - while, in the case of through traffic from the Cromford Canal to the Peak Forest Canal, public hauliers were available if required. The railway company's angle was, of course, that it charged the private and public users for passing over the line - similar, in fact, to how Railtrack works today!

Despite the enthusiasm and optimism which had accompanied the promotion of the railway, before very long the harsh reality of operational life provided something of a dampener. One of the C&HPR's problems was the difficulty of transporting an adequate amount of traffic, the line's traffic capacity (i.e. its revenue-earning capability) being effectively dictated by the speed with which the inclines could be negotiated. It will be noted that Jessop's report of 1824 estimated a revenue based on 153,000 tons of traffic passing over the C&HPR annually. This was equivalent to 500 tons - i.e. over eighty 6-ton wagons - per working day, which would have necessitated two runs per hour on every incline, throughout each working day. It was theoretically possible, but it

was a rather tall order. Furthermore, in those days of nine inclines, congestion or a delay at any one of them had a knock-on effect throughout the line - indeed, a journey from Cromford Wharf to Whaley Bridge could take *two days* - though, of course, at that time there was no faster alternative. The problem of negotiating the inclines with adequate speed was made even more difficult in 1833 when, following a runaway, the number of wagons handled simultaneously at an incline was limited to just *two* in each direction.

Another problem encountered by the C&HPR was a form of price war - rival canal companies reduced their tolls, and so the railway company had to do likewise. Inevitably, the customers benefited from the struggle, and the C&HPR correspondence books reveal countless instances of customers threatening to take their goods by some other means unless the railway company offered a special reduction in rates. In many cases the C&HPR gave way.

Before very long the company found itself in financial trouble, and by 1842 it was in debt to the tune of almost £47,000. Much of that was accounted for by unpaid bills (and interest thereon) for the line's construction some twelve years or so earlier. Despite a financial restructuring in 1843, the C&HPR still needed to explore all avenues for potential economies. For example, on 5 December 1844 the C&HPR General Manager, John Leonard, was instructed to: '.....regulate the hours of working the first and last inclined planes so as to economise on the coal without causing any inconvenience to the traders'.

Several reasons for the C&HPR's financial plight have already been given, but the company's position was not helped by an apparent corporate inability to realise that the lull wasn't just temporary. Many of the company's actions smacked of 'making do until things improve'. For

example, the company's readiness to reduce its rates seemed not to take into account the basic fact that there was, inevitably, a limit below which the company could not economically go. According to the C&HPR's own figures the cost of working of the nine inclined planes added up to one shilling per ton but, to quote one instance at random, in 1845 Messrs. D.Wheatcroft secured a reduction on through traffic - i.e. all the way between Cromford and Whaley Bridge - from 2/8d to 2/- per ton. If 1/- of that was accounted for by working the inclines, only 1/- was left to cover the costs of working the rest of the line. It could hardly have been profitable for the C&HPR.

It has been argued elsewhere that the C&HPR's financial position was hampered by its total isolation, for the first 23 years of its life, from the rest of Britain's railway network - it remained unconnected to any other railway until 1853. However, one might ask what benefit a connection would have been. The C&HPR seemingly had problems enough with its existing traffic (capacity being dictated by the inclines and, to a lesser extent, by a seemingly eternal shortage of wagons) and so, if a connection to the outside world brought in additional traffic, the company wasn't in too good a position to accommodate it. Whatever the case, the C&HPR's isolation came to an end on 21 February 1853 when a one-mile long spur was opened between Cromford Wharf and the recently opened Manchester, Buxton, Matlock & Midlands Junction Railway (latterly more familiar as the Ambergate-Rowsley line).

The connection to the outside world seemed to jolt the C&HPR into seeking a long-term solution to its problems. The company undertook another major financial and administrative restructuring, which culminated in its formal reincorporation on 26 June 1855. One important aspect of the restructuring was that, for the first

The top of Middleton Incline, almost 1,000ft above sea level, on 31 May 1959. In the distance, behind the engine house, is prominent evidence of the railway's staple traffic - stone. There was extensive quarrying, principally for limestone, along much of the route. PHOTOGRAPH: NEVILLE STEAD

time, it was able to act as a public carrier - as explained earlier, traffic passing over the line had previously been worked by private traders or contractors using their own horses and wagons. However, the C&HPR's new powers in this respect did not result in an overnight transformation, as until the early 1860s - by which time the company had its own locomotives - much of the traffic was still being worked by private traders using their own horses and wagons.

Another important aspect of the C&HPR's restructuring was that with the aid of new financial powers, the directors confidently proposed a series of swingeing improvements to the line. The company appointed Captain William Moorsom to inspect and report on the proposed improvements. Moorsom was not without his critics - the engineer and writer, Francis Conder, described a 'Captain Transom' (a thinly veiled Capt. Moorsom) as 'a man too full of contradictions to be dismissed in a line' and 'perhaps difficult to be judged with fairness'. Those opinions were based largely on the fact that Moorsom had obtained responsible engineering positions with at least two major railway companies despite his lack of suitable experience. It was considered that he had landed the posts due to a combination of his own bluff and his employers' naiveté. Perhaps the most damning comment about Moorsom was that he had taken to Parliament more railway bills than almost any other engineer of the day, and had lost all but one of them. His only success, it was claimed, had been due solely to the exertions of the contractor who had been engaged to build the line. That success was for the Birmingham & Gloucester's route via the Lickey Incline - a line which caused operational problems for a century and a quarter! But we digress......

Moorsom's report was presented at the first directors' meeting of the 'new' C&HPR (chaired by Francis Wright of Osmaston Manor, near Derby)

on 8 August 1855. One section of his report concerned proposed improvements to the northern part of the line: '....a new or deviated line of railway, from a point north of the Buxton tunnel to the top of the first Whaley incline.....'. This proposed new line, originally estimated to cost £3,988, was to be on a uniform gradient of 1 in 60, albeit on a very twisting descent - its principal purpose was to avoid Bunsall and Shallcross Inclines completely. However, the new line was strongly opposed by the Manchester, Sheffield & Lincolnshire Railway, which had its own plans to reach Buxton, and so the C&HPR withdrew rather than be faced with costly legal battles.

Although that proposal was dropped, the C&HPR pursued another plan for: '.....an extended line to form a junction with the Stockport, Disley and Whaley Bridge Railway'. The SD&WBR was a subsidiary of the LNWR, and was a component in what ultimately became the Manchester-Buxton-Ashbourne line. It opened between Stockport and Whaley Bridge on 9 June 1857, and the C&HPR's connection to the new line at the latter point was brought into use a little over two months later, on 17 August. The C&HPR attached great importance to its relationship with the SD&WBR, and had invested £3,740 in it and appointed one director to its board. Nevertheless, the C&HPR's directors emphasised that they had: '....no wish to interfere in the internal affairs of the Stockport & Disley Company, but..... there must ultimately be a great communication between the two Companies.....'

Returning to the year 1855, another part of Capt. Moorsom's report concerned proposed alterations to the method of working some of the inclines. At the south-eastern end of the line, Cromford and Sheep Pasture inclines were worked as separate entities, as were the two adjacent inclines at Bunsall (referred to in some official documents as 'Buxton'), on the northern part of the line, and the C&HP considered that, by combining

each pair of inclines, the working of the entire line could be improved. Moorsom reported on 8 August 1855 that he had: '.....calculated with some anxiety the power and also the applicability of the present stationary engines at Cromford and Buxton (Bunsall) inclines for working each of those spots when converted each into one incline. I find that by employing both engines equal to 40 horse power at the top of each spot, the traffic will be efficiently conveyed to the same extent as at present - that is to say in loads not exceeding 24 tons at a speed of about seven miles per hour. I have assumed each engine to be equal to 20 horse power'.

Moorsom was also required to look at 'the provision of locomotives and their stables'. He reported that: 'The sum estimated for two engines and tenders was £3,800, and I have offers from good makers to supply two engines and tenders for £2,000'. (It seems that these engines were not actually purchased). The final section of Moorsom's report concerned the proposed replacement of the permanent way: 'I feel satisfied that you (the C&HPR) will not carry the traffic which your district can command in a satisfactory manner until you have replaced with wrought iron rails the present cast iron ones for, at all events, the greater part of the entire line .....every yard of your line so replaced is of the utmost importance to the security and efficiency of your traffic'.

It was soon learned that a supply of second-hand rails was available from the GWR, and on 21 August 1855 the C&HPR's directors resolved that: 'Captain Moorsom be authorised to arrange with the agents of the Great Western Railway for the purchase of not more than 1,000 tons of rails ('best selected rails', delivered to Bulls Bridge, near Ambergate - a somewhat curious point of delivery, perhaps - at a rate of £5.10s per ton) provided that on inspection they be found suitable for the traffic of this railway'. A later report (dated 25 September 1856) referred to a supply of second-hand rails being available for inspection at Waterford but, tantalisingly, no further details are given as to their original source.

Hard Times - Again

Things might have sounded rather promising, but problems were never very far away. Despite the C&HPR's corporate restructuring, there was still insufficient money available for all the proposed improvements which, even excluding the replacement of the rails, were estimated at almost £16,000. On 26 September 1855 the C&HPR gloomily announced that 'moneys expended and owing' amounted to over £14,500 - this included a £2,100 bill for wagons from the Butterley Company, £216 for a wire hauling rope, £300 for buildings at Whaley Bridge, and £3,400 for 4,800yds of rails and fitments for four inclined planes. (Those rails, incidentally, were quoted by the C&HPR as being a hefty *112lb* per yard - are we overlooking something obvious here?). A small part of the company's outlay on replacement rails was eventually recouped, some of the old rails being sold - among the purchasers was the Butterley Co., which was charged £3.12s.6d per ton.

As for the C&HPR's inability to carry out its proposed improvements, this would have caused a small degree of satisfaction to the LNWR. The mighty LNWR had, in a somewhat alarmist manner, expressed concern that: '.....if the character of the C&HPR line were to be made first class so as to run through trains at high speeds, it would become a competitor to the LNWR; but while the C&HPR remains a second- or third-class railway making such speeds as 16 to 20 miles per hour, it should be an auxiliary to the LNWR, which the LNWR would encourage by all fair means'. The LNWR had nothing to fear, as the C&HPR was not to become a 'first class, high speed' route.

The C&HPR's prompt return to penury was discussed by the directors on 30 January 1856: '.....regret to state that the proprietors in general have not taken that interest in the Company by subscribing for the new capital .....of the £20,000 authorised only £13,960 has been subscribed, and that by the directors themselves .....the only alterations at present commenced have been on converting the two inclined planes at Cromford into one, and also the two inclines near Buxton (Bunsall). When these alterations are completed the inclines will be worked by wire ropes, two stationary engines will be dispensed with, and a saving effected of nearly £600 a year.....'. (Those improvements to the northern section of the line were in lieu of the new avoiding line to Whaley Bridge, the plans for which had been dropped in 1855).

One of the casualties of the C&HPR's resultant economy drive was Capt. Moorsom as, with the suspension of new works on the line, the services of a resident engineer were deemed superfluous. Moorsom was paid off in August 1856, but remained available for consultancy work.

There was, however, at least some cause for optimism, the directors noting that: 'As soon as the warehouse (the Peak Forest Canal Co.'s warehouse at Whaley Bridge) is completed we hope to regain a considerable share of the Flour Traffic which has been lost to us for many years from the want of accommodation. Steps are now being taken to regain this trade, and applications are also being made to Messrs. Strutt and to Mr.Salt, which will, we hope, result in our obtaining the carrying of considerable quantities of cotton for Belper and ale for Buxton.'

Things seemed to have improved a little by 1857, the directors reporting on 30 July of that year that the company's revenue during the last half year had increased by £148.18s.3d, 'arising principally from minerals'. By this time the con-

nection with the new SD&WBR line at Whaley Bridge was at an advanced stage, and there was much hope that it would, by providing a direct through communication between the Midland Railway and the LNWR, bring about a considerable increase in traffic. As some of the improvements to the northern end of the C&HP line had been completed by this time - Shallcross Incline had been equipped with new ropes in May and the two inclines at Bunsall had been combined in June - the C&HPR was in a far better position to handle additional traffic. In practice, however, a shortage of wagons - and the money to purchase any additional wagons - proved to be a problem.

Another possible problem surfaced on 27 July 1857 when the SD&WBR obtained powers to extend its line to Buxton. The threat of head-on competition was, however, avoided, the C&HPR directors reporting on 'satisfactory arrangements' with the SD&WBR 'by which the injury the Company otherwise would have sustained had been obviated'. The precise nature of the 'satisfactory arrangements' is unclear, although a later report referred to the agreement of non-competitive rates for coal and minerals, and a payment of £3,000 from the SD&WBR to the C&HPR 'to enable them to make the necessary works at Whaley (Bridge)'. The SD&WBR's Buxton extension - which actually necessitated alterations to the C&HPR alignment at Whaley Bridge - opened to the public on 15 June 1863. By this time, though, there had been radical changes on the C&HPR.

A New Administration

The first hint of the changes had been heard on 25 February 1858 when the C&HPR's directors, facing further financial difficulties, had resolved that: '.....powers be sought to lease or sell the Line to the London & North Western, or Midland, or Stockport & Disley, or Manchester Sheffield & Lincolnshire

The J94 'Austerity' 0-6-0STs monopolised the workings on the Middleton Top - Friden section from 1960 onwards. This is No.68012, which was transferred to the C&HPR in September 1959, departed in September 1960, but returned in April 1962 to remain until the closure of the line in 1967. Wearing a neglected air, it waits at Middleton Top before departing with the Friden goods on 19 June 1965. PHOTOGRAPH: DEREK CROSS

Railway Companies, or some or one of them'. It was, however, over three years before there were firm developments. The interested party was the LNWR, who took a lease on the line, commencing on 1 April 1861. (The date of the commencement of the lease is quoted in *Bradshaw's Shareholders' Guide* as 25 March - our date comes from C&HPR documents).

In mid-March - a couple of weeks or so before the lease came into effect - the C&HPR directors had stressed that their company was 'entitled to take away the old rails, old stationary engines and other stores or materials out of use'. The lease was not formally ratified until 30 June 1862 - it stipulated a rent of £3,500 for the first year and £4,000 for subsequent years. The ensuing transitional period did not please everybody - for example, a C&HPR directors' minute noted that: *'The Secretary reported that he had received a notice from the London & North Western Co. to quit his house and offices at Michaelmas next....'*

The LNWR soon undertook a number of improvements to the C&HPR. These included a deviation to avoid Hurdlow Incline (opened 4 January 1869), the straightening of the route between Harpur Hill and Ladmanlow (*circa* 1875 - these improvements had been proposed in the mid-1850s by the C&HPR), and the switch from a stationary engine to locomotive traction on Hopton Incline (this change was made in 1877, but possibly more of necessity than anything else). With the elimination of the stationary engine at Hopton Incline and the deviation to avoid Hurdlow Incline it became possible to use locomotive power all the way between Middleton Top and Bunsall Top, thereby enabling a significant improvement to be made in journey times from one end of the line to the other. In 1877 the LNWR proposed an amalgamation with the C&HPR, offering £100,000 in discharge of the annual rent. This offer was discussed by the C&HPR's directors on 12 December, but was rejected on the grounds that no stock was included - they wanted a sum of £104,000 'in lieu of Debenture Stock'. Although the difference was proportionately small it took ten years before terms were agreed, and with the LNWR agreeing to give 4% debenture stock to C&HP shareholders, amalgamation finally took place on 1 July 1887. (The date is quoted elsewhere as 19 July - we have taken our date from C&HPR documents). The C&HPR might have ceased to exist in name, but the railway itself was to remain known as the High Peak Railway for the rest of its eighty-year existence.

As the sole proprietors of the High Peak line, the LNWR undertook further improvements and alterations to the railway during the 1890s. The biggest change of all was undoubtedly that of the northern section of the line. After the last train had passed on Saturday 25 June 1892 the Ladmanlow-Shallcross section closed completely, and a new connection between Dowlow and the LNWR at Buxton was brought into use in time for the commencement of traffic on the following Monday, 27 June. This new arrangement enabled northbound traffic from the Ladmanlow end of the High Peak line to be taken via Buxton, rather than having to negotiate the three inclines on the old alignment. This was a huge improvement. Also on 27 June, a much revised alignment between Hindlow and Ladmanlow was brought into use, further aiding the speedier passage of traffic on the Ladmanlow section.

Despite the closure of the Ladmanlow-Shallcross section in June 1892, the northern extremity of the High Peak line - Shallcross Yard (at the bottom of the incline) to the canal wharves at Whaley Bridge - remained open. This section included Whaley Bridge Incline, which was to remain operational until April 1952 (worked by a horse-operated capstan until the very end), while Shallcross Yard was to continue in use until 30 January 1965.

Reverting to the 1890s, on 1 June 1894 a passenger service was introduced between Buxton and Parsley Hay, the Hindlow-Parsley Hay section having been doubled for this purpose, and on 4 August 1899 the LNWR opened its new line between Parsley Hay and Ashbourne to passenger traffic. This gave the LNWR a through run from Manchester to Ashbourne, and an end-on connection with the North Staffordshire Railway at the latter point provided a link to Burton, Derby and beyond.

Despite the various improvements, the Middleton-Parsley Hay section was left with its proliferation of sharp curves - when the line had been built, the curves had been considered preferable to extensive and costly engineering works. The Longcliffe-Friden section alone had no less than twenty-one curves of five chains or under, the sharpest being Gotham Curve, which had a 2½ chain (55yd) radius - believed to be the sharpest on any British standard gauge running line. The curves prevented anything other than four-wheeled wagons from being used south of Friden. This was one of the many factors which, in later years especially, hampered economical operation. The proprietors of the High Peak line were not unaware of

Despite the various improvements undertaken by the LNWR, it was not practicable to ease Gotham Curve, a little to the north-west of Minninglow. The curve had a radius of only 2½ chains (55yds), and was the sharpest on any running line in Britain. No.68012 and a modest train negotiate the curve, heading towards Friden on 12 July 1966. PHOTOGRAPH: IVO PETERS

the problem - in 1890 the LNWR proposed a completely new avoiding line, some 3¹/2 miles long, from the bottom of Middleton Incline to a point to the west of Hopton Top (thereby circumventing the two inclines completely), but the proposal was dropped after ferocious opposition from quarry owners in the Hopton and Middleton areas, who would have lost their direct rail connections.

After the improvements of the 1890s, the High Peak Railway settled down to a relatively uneventful existence. At the grouping in 1923 it became part of the LMSR, but this did not bring about any immediate changes to working practices - the line had specialised requirements and was, to a degree, self-contained, and so any major changes would have been akin to trying to mend something that wasn't broken. That said, there was an on-going programme of sorts to upgrade the equipment and the like, although largely due to the line's goods only status and 'out of the way' nature, any improvements were usually undertaken with economy to the fore, and normally involved second-hand equipment and materials. One example was seen in 1925 when parts of the High Peak line were relayed with rails which had been recovered from the ex-LNWR main line.

During the LMS era, the High Peak line suffered one of its most unfortunate incidents, a fatal accident near Hopton Incline on 6 October 1937. The accident involved the 8.35am goods from Middleton to Parsley Hay, which comprised four loaded wagons and a 20-ton brake and was hauled by ex-North London Railway 0-6-0T, then LMS No.27521, one of a type which had made its debut on the High Peak line in 1931. The engine was in the charge of Driver William 'Billy' Boden (who was fatally injured) and Fireman Harold Kirk (seriously injured), with goods guards Herbert Slack and Tom Swift and numbertaker J.Spence (all of whom received injuries) in the brake van. The whole of the train left the rails at the foot of Hopton Incline; it was apparently travelling at a speed of about 45 miles an hour, preparatory to 'rushing' the gradient, as was common practice. The engine, three of the wagons, and the brake van rolled down a 25ft embankment, coming to rest in a public road and being seriously damaged. The remaining wagon, originally the leading wagon of the train, was derailed towards the opposite side of the track, and remained on the embankment.

For the record, although Hopton Incline was famous for its 1 in 14 gradient (hence the usual practice of 'rushing' the approach), the initial approach to the foot of the incline was actually *down* a gradient of 1 in 1056; the ascent commenced at 1 in 60, steepening first to 1 in 20 and then to 1 in 14 in its upper half. The incline itself was straight, but its foot was approached over a curvature of about 20 chains radius, right-handed for ascending trains, and was 160 yards or thereabouts in length. The curve, on which the derailment originated, was on the 1 in 1,056 falling gradient.

The Ministry of Transport routinely investigated the cause of the accident, Lt-Col Woodhouse noting in his report of 17 December: *'The weather was fine and there had been no rain for some weeks beforehand. The track had been relayed in 1925 .....normally there are 12 sleepers per rail length, but on the curve in question the number has been increased to 13 per rail, to strengthen the track, and heavier sleepers (12ins by 6ins) have been used. The chairs are secured by two screws and two spikes. Ballast is of ash, and the track is rated as third class for maintenance purposes'.*

The prime cause of the derailment was that the track on the approach to the incline had spread by about 3° inches for a distance of some 27 feet, but the investigating officer had to determine what had caused the spreading in the first place. In customary fashion, the official report described the working practices on the line. It noted that prior to 1936 there had been no recommended speed limits for locomotives anywhere on the High Peak line, but in that year a speed limit of 30mph had been introduced for the entire length of the line, albeit with the exception of the approach to Hopton Incline, which remained unrestricted so as to allow the practice of 'rushing' the incline to continue. It was also noted by the Ministry Inspector that the immediate approach to the incline was on a 20-chain curve which had a cant of six inches - rushing the slope on such a curve without any sort of camber would, of course, have been all but impossible.

During the enquiry evidence was given by Driver Tom Walker, who had been driving on the High Peak line for 21 years. He stated that it was his practice to go 'all out' from Hopton Tunnel, which was about three furlongs short of the curve, and he estimated that his speed on the curve was usually about 40mph, rising to 50mph on the short length of straight track between the curve and the incline. Driver Walker added that he had often failed to get to the top of the incline at the first attempt.

Driver Walker opined that the NLR tank engines tended to run roughly, '.....appearing to surge from side to side, and that at times it seemed as if the track was moving with them'. He added that, on wet or greasy rails, they seemed to go round a curve in a series of lurches, although their running in dry weather was satisfactory. (It had been dry when the accident had occurred). Walker also stated that the NLR tanks were harder on the road than the old Webb 'Choppers' - the 2-4-0Ts which had been used on the line since the 1890s.

Another opinion about the NLR tanks was obtained from Fireman Kirk, who had been firing No.27521 at the time of the accident. Kirk, who could not be interviewed until 26 November on account of the injuries he had received, considered that the engines oscillated rather violently at high speed, the one involved in the accident being '.....rather worse in this respect than the others on the line', and that on the run up to Hopton Incline the oscillation '.....usually became noticeable on the curve, and continued until a point about 150yds up the gradient was reached'. In the ensuing report, the Ministry Inspector emphasised that the North London tanks '.....embodying a short rigid wheelbase, long overhang, and outside cylinders.....' were not suitable for running at high speed, and that the oscillation was '.....what might have been expected from an engine of this type running fast and working hard'. During the enquiry Fireman Kirk stated that, on the day of the accident, as soon as the train reached the curve he '.....felt the road give under the engine, which made the engine rock about more than usual', but he was unable to recall whether his driver had seemed alarmed when this had happened.

The locomotive involved in the accident had been dismantled on site and taken to Derby for close examination. Excluding accident damage, no serious defects were discovered. Similarly, the wagons - or, in one case, what was left of it - had revealed nothing untoward. Furthermore, the train had been within the loading limit of six wagons. When the North London tanks had first been tried

on the High Peak line they had proved capable of hauling nine loaded wagons up Hopton Incline, but in order to allow for unfavourable conditions the official limit had been set at seven. That had later been reduced to six as, in the words of the LMSR District Inspector: '.....if an engine failed to get to the top with seven, much time was wasted in setting back for a second attempt'. There was, however, a variable in all this. The High Peak line traversed an area of limestone, and during a prolonged period of dry weather (as had been the case before the accident) the quality of the local water supply was affected. In the case of the water available for locomotives, a deterioration in quality could increase the risk of priming which, of course, would affect a loco's ability to climb Hopton Incline with even a 'legal' load.

The other main factor in the equation was the track. During the official investigation, Fireman Kirk and others explained that the track on the curve sometimes got out of line, particularly in wet weather, but whenever that had occurred the permanent way men had attended to it very promptly. The ganger in charge of the line explained that the curve was constantly monitored - rail piles (old rails about 3ft long) were driven into the formation at the ends of the sleepers at intervals around the curve to check for lateral movement. It was agreed by all concerned that the track had been in good order prior to the accident, the routine inspection that very morning having revealed no distortion or settlement, nor any loose chair keys. The track was ballasted with ash which, in the dry weather, was slightly less cohesive that might have been desired, but it was not considered that this had any significant bearing on events. The track displacement, which had been the direct cause of the accident had, in the opinion of the Ministry Inspector, been caused by the oscillation of the engine and the corresponding sinuous movement in the train.

Having identified the primary cause of the accident, Lt-Col Woodhouse, concluded that it had resulted from an '.....unfortunate combination of circumstances, viz., an engine travelling over ash ballasted track, possibly unusually lacking in lateral stability, at a speed for which its design rendered it unsuitable'. He noted that the LMSR had proposed to realign and adjust the curve on the approach to Hopton Incline, but he suggested that, whether or not that was actually carried out, '.....the lateral stability of the track approaching the foot of the incline should be improved by the use of a better class of ballast than ash'. It was also noted that, since the accident, a speed restriction of 35mph had been imposed on the section around the curve, and that 'unlimited' speed was now permitted only on the short length of straight track between the curve and the foot of the incline. Tests had been conducted under those restrictions, and it had been decided to reduce the load for the North London tanks to just four wagons on the incline. Heavier trains would have to be divided and taken up in two parts.

..........ooo..........

During World War II the C&HPR played no little part in the war effort, several of the factories along its route supplying minerals which were used in the manufacture of steel, explosives and fertilisers. A few years later - on 1 January 1948 - the Cromford & High Peak line became part of British Railways. The story of how the line fared under BR ownership continues later.....

2....The Route

The goods shed at Cromford Wharf, June 1962. The running line from High Peak Junction passes under the loading gauge, and the road on the right (where the car is parked) leads up to the A6 trunk road. PHOTOGRAPH: E.R.MORTEN

'.....the Beer House at Longcliffe is let to Mr.Frost and the company receives five pounds per annum rent.....'

Initially, the southernmost extremity of the C&HPR was at Cromford Wharf, but in February 1853 the line was extended for a little over three quarters of a mile to the Ambergate-Rowsley main line, which it joined at the appropriately named **High Peak Junction**, about a mile north of Whatstandwell station. The connecting line between the C&HPR and High Peak Junction was single track, and was bordered on one side, firstly by the Cromford Canal, and then by the River Derwent, and on the other side by the Derby-Buxton trunk road (A6). From a point 500 yards from High Peak Junction the line was worked as a siding, and from that point to Cromford Wharf by means of a train staff. The line ascended steadily in the direction of **Cromford Wharf**, having a ruling gradient of 1 in 120.

In the C&HPR's early years, in particular, the wharf on the Cromford Canal was vital to the company's business - after all, the railway had been conceived principally as a means of connection to/ from the Peak Forest Canal at Whaley Bridge. However, by the late 1840s the nationwide economic slump, combined with various forms of more localised competition - new railways and canals - resulted in a gradual, but irreversible, decline in the use of the canal. Nevertheless, it ultimately became part of the Midland Railway and remained operational until 1900 when a serious collapse in Butterley Tunnel resulted in it being bisected at that point. Cromford Wharf was on the isolated section of the canal and so its original function was more or less nullified.

As already emphasised, the presence of inclined planes on the C&HPR effectively divided the line into separate sections. Because of this a

locomotive or two was outstationed semi-permanently on each section and, consequently, each section had its own engine shed. The locomotive used on shunting duties between Cromford and High Peak Junction was accommodated in a shed adjacent to the canal. It is believed that the building was converted, circa 1860, from the C&HPR's former chain shop - in the company's early years haulage chains and other engineering supplies were brought in by canal boat, hence the structure's opening and canopy on the canal side. In later years a timber extension was added to the northern end of the shed.

On leaving Cromford Wharf, 277ft above sea level, the railway immediately had to rise 465ft in just three quarters of a mile. This was accomplished by means of the first of the famous inclines - **Cromford Incline** and **Sheep Pasture Incline.** These were originally two separate features, Cromford being 580 yards at 1 in 9 and Sheep Pasture 711 yards at 1 in 8, with a short level section between them, but in 1857 the two inclines were combined as one, with an overall length of 1,320 yards. When worked separately each had its own hauling engine (jet condensing type, boiler pressure 2½psi, two cylinders 25inch diameter and 60 inch stroke, and rated at 40hp), but the combining of the inclines enabled the lower engine to be dispensed with.

The machinery in the engine houses was not indestructible, nor was remedial work easy, a memo of 7 August 1837 referring to Cromford Upper Engine (Sheep Pasture): *'....accident in breaking the chainwheel .....new one ordered from the Butterley Iron Co. .....it will be necessary to cast the chain wheel (14ft 1in in diameter) in four parts to get it into the engine house.....'* In 1856, when the C&HPR was optimistically looking to undertake wholesale improvements all along the line, Mr.Edward Reynolds of the Butterley Iron Co. was requested to inspect all the stationary engines and

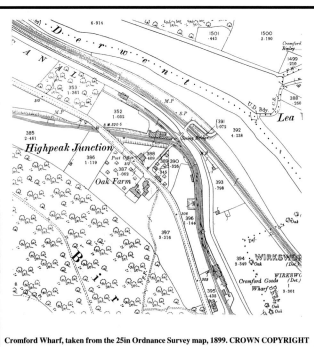

Cromford Wharf, taken from the 25in Ordnance Survey map, 1899. CROWN COPYRIGHT

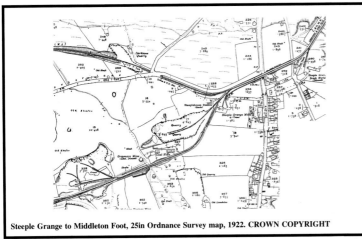

Steeple Grange to Middleton Foot, 25in Ordnance Survey map, 1922. CROWN COPYRIGHT

report on their condition. His report, dated 25 February, noted of the Sheep Pasture engine: '*Cylinders require reboring, one cylinder bottom broken, air pumps so bad that it is doubtful whether they would bear reboring. The boilers are worn out. Engine requires reversing gear to be fitted to it. One new piston wanted. Approximate cost or repairs - delivery of whole at Cromford Wharf and erection of the new and repaired work: £560.*' (That estimate included adapting some of the equipment from the Cromford engine, which was about to be made redundant by the combining of the two inclines).

In 1884 the Sheep Pasture engine was replaced by one which had been converted from a Ramsbottom DX 0-6-0, steam being received at 60psi. It might have looked a little unorthodox, but it was wholly effective. Another departure from convention came in 1965 when the old DX boiler at Sheep Pasture was replaced by a 100hp electric motor. New steel pulleys were also installed. This might have seemed rather late in the day for such modernisation, but at the time a respectable amount of quarry traffic was still being brought down from Middleton Quarry. Even with the new equipment, ascending and descending loads were balanced whenever possible, but if necessary out-of-balance loads of 60 tons (downwards) or 10 tons (upwards) could be handled.

The working of the inclines was not without its problems. The instance of runaway wagons was far from unknown, and after a particularly spectacular runaway on Cromford/ Sheep Pasture Incline in 1888 it was decided to install a runaway pit there. The pit was between the tracks near the bottom, and runaways could be directed into the pit by means of catch points - the points were actually kept 'open' for the pit, and it required a positive action from the pointsman to set the points for a normal descent. The pointsman was alerted to a runaway by means of gongs. Some distance above the points were two gongs operated by treadles - if the gongs sounded at normal intervals everything was satisfactory, but if they rang too quickly something was amiss and so the pointsman left the points set for the pit and made a hasty exit to the other side of the wall.

The working instructions for the railway stipulated that while an incline was in operation (this applied to *all* the inclines) locomotives were not permitted to stand within 100 yards of the foot of the incline. Each of the inclines was laid with double track, but apart from passing loops and sidings etc, the 'level' sections of the C&HPR were single track only.

At **Sheep Pasture Top** (1³/₄ miles from High Peak Junction), an engine shed was provided for the locomotive working between there and Middleton Foot. The original shed, believed to have been built of timber, was replaced sometime before 1920 by a longer corrugated iron structure, but that was destroyed by a gale in 1962. Duties on the Sheep Pasture-Middleton section were usually lighter than elsewhere on the C&HPR line, and so older or less powerful locomotives were normally

outstationed there. From Sheep Pasture Top, the C&HPR continued almost on the level for a little over 1¹/₄ miles to the foot of Middleton Incline. This section was liberally sprinkled with quarry workings, a number of which had siding connections, but several of the quarries had fairly brief operational lives and their sidings were abandoned or removed. In later years, the principal working in the immediate area was **Middleton Quarry**, which was served by a ³/₄-mile long branch. This was the property of the quarry company, but was worked by the regular Sheep Pasture-Middleton locomotive. The branch joined the C&HPR 'main line' near **Steeplehouse Goods Depot,** one of several public goods 'stations' on the C&HPR.

One little mystery about this part of the C&HPR concerns various references in early documents to 'Wirksworth Wharf' - given that Steeplehouse Goods was not too far from the town of Wirksworth, and that Wirksworth didn't have a railway of its own until 1867 (when the Midland Railway branch opened), could it be that the C&HPR regarded Steeplehouse Goods as the nominal staging point for Wirksworth? An alternative - and more likely - candidate for the title of 'Wirksworth Wharf' was **Middlepeak Goods Yard**, which was only the proverbial stone's throw from the community of Wirksworth and was served by a short branch from near the foot of Middleton Incline. Despite its grandiose title, Middlepeak Goods Yard comprised little more than a few sidings.

An interesting feature near the foot of Middleton Incline were earthworks, built for a connection between the C&HPR and the Midland Railway Wirksworth branch. This connection - which was intended to have been worked by stationary engine - was never actually laid with rails, let alone brought into use, and from around the 1920s was gradually quarried away.

The next landmark along the route was **Middleton Incline**, 708 yards long and on a gradient of 1 in 8¹/₂. The winding engine was a two cylinder low-pressure condensing engine rated at 40hp, virtually identical to those at Cromford and Sheep Pasture, and its condition was reported on by Edward Reynolds in February 1856: '*One of the cylinders has a hole through it, and the other wants new bottom and valve casing. The condition of the air pumps is uncertain. Both the boilers are in a very bad state. Approximate cost of repairs, including delivering and erecting the whole: £680.*'

In 1857, a siding was laid from the incline itself to Wheatcroft's quarry, and this meant allotting one of the two tracks on the incline exclusively for quarry usage. For C&HP purposes, the incline was, therefore, reduced to single track, and this entailed considerable alterations to the method of working the incline. The quarry was not particularly long lived, but the incline did not revert to double line operation until 1894, the winding engine being 're-adapted' at a cost of £1,300, using materials salvaged from the engines at Bunsall and Shallcross, which had been made redundant in 1892.

By 1959 the boiler of the Middleton engine was in dire condition, and so an old Ramsbottom DX boiler, converted for stationary use and mounted on the underframe of one of the water tanks, was brought in. This did not prove to be a long-term solution, as the old locomotive boiler was condemned only a few years on. By then, much of the traffic on the C&HPR originated near Middleton Foot and was taken out via Sheep Pasture Incline, and it was therefore considered that Middleton Incline could be closed, thus circumventing the cost

The mess room at Cromford Wharf was an old LNWR coach body. The canal can be seen just behind. 25 April 1953. PHOTOGRAPH: F.W. SHUTTLEWORTH, COURTESY INDUSTRIAL RAILWAY SOCIETY

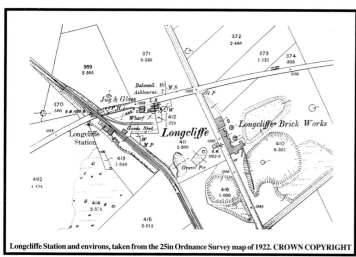

Longcliffe Station and environs, taken from the 25in Ordnance Survey map of 1922. CROWN COPYRIGHT

of replacing the boiler. An engine shed was provided at **Middleton Top** for the locomotives working onwards from there. It is assumed that this shed was built in 1877 when locomotive working between Middleton Top and Bunsall was introduced. The original structure was in timber, but was destroyed by fire in July 1905. At the time of the fire two 'Choppers', LNWR Nos.2244 and 2278, were inside the shed and despite being somewhat carbonised, they were repairable. Indeed, No.2278 lasted until 1952 - as BR No.58092 it was the last survivor of the class. The replacement shed was built of corrugated iron. The water supply at Middleton was by means of tenders - these were brought in and discharged into an adjacent reservoir, the water then being pumped into the water tank.

On reaching the top of Middleton Incline the railway was close to the 1,000ft contour - it had climbed over 700ft since leaving Cromford Wharf. From Middleton Top the line continued on a ruling gradient of 1 in 1056 (falling) for three quarters of a mile towards Hopton. On that section was the 113-yard **Hopton Tunnel**, while near the foot of Hopton Incline a three quarter mile long branch diverged to **Hopton Wood Stone Quarries**. That branch opened circa 1850, and from 1857 or thereabouts was worked by a stationary engine, situated at the point where the quarry

branch joined the 'main line'. Also near the foot of Hopton Incline was a siding serving a bone works, but by the 1930s the premises were reported to be derelict. In 1963 the Magnesium Elektron works were established on the site of the old bone factory and the siding facility was resuscitated, but the works closed in 1966, having generated negligible traffic for the railway.

Hopton Incline

- built on a gradient of 1 in 14 for 457 yards - was originally worked by a 20hp stationary engine (probably also of the jet condensing type), but in April 1877 conventional adhesion working was introduced. It is widely considered that the switch to locomotive working was prompted by the poor condition of the winding engine which, by then, was virtually fifty years old. In 1852, Edward Reynolds had reported: *'One valve casing broken. Other parts supposed to be in fair order. New packing rings for slide valves wanted. One boiler very bad. Repairs, delivery and erection: £260.'* Prior to the introduction of locomotives on the incline, there was an engine shed at Hopton Top - it housed the locomotive(s) engaged on the Hopton-Bunsall section.

For some thirty-odd years after the introduction of conventional locomotive working on Hopton Incline, the gradient remained unaltered. The 1 in 14 was claimed to be the steepest gradient in Britain routinely worked by adhesion. (There were other claimants for the 'steepest in Britain' title - for example, a 150-yard stretch of 1 in 13 on Bakers Bank on the Tanfield Railway in County Durham was very occasionally worked by adhesion. To the best of this author's knowledge, though, Hopton Incline was the steepest to be *routinely* worked by adhesion). In the early 1900s - after

various proposals had been made but not acted upon - the approach to the foot of the incline was remodelled with a 200-yard section of 1 in 16, then 75 yards at 1 in 30, followed by 100 yards at 1 in 20, which reduced the 1 in 14 section to 200 yards. But it was still a ferocious gradient, and it was far from uncommon for a locomotive to stall on the incline and to require a couple of attempts before a successful ascent was achieved. Inevitably, the usual practice was for crews to 'rush' the incline - this practice was accepted by officialdom, and when a 30mph speed limit was introduced for the line in the 1930s the section approaching the foot of Hopton Incline remained unrestricted. (The 30mph limit was, more or less, for official purposes only - under normal circumstances there was precious little hope of attaining such a heady speed anywhere on the C&HPR).

To the unsuspecting, the sight of a small tank engine and a rake of loose coupled wagons charging around the bend in readiness to rush the incline might have seemed somewhat hair-raising, but it looked far more precarious than it actually was. That said, as related earlier, on 6 October 1937 a locomotive and its train derailed near Hopton Foot, killing the driver. Sometimes, ascending trains were double-headed, while on other occasions a single-headed train was taken up the incline in two parts, the first set of wagons being held in a siding at the top of the incline. In its rope-worked days, incidentally, Hopton Incline had two tracks. The second track fell into disuse around the time locomotive working was introduced, but was not lifted until the early 1900s - probably during the alterations to the incline. The rails on the incline were relayed in 1961 - apparently 'in anticipation of increased traffic'.

Hopton Top marked the change of a train staff section - the two sections concerned were Middleton Top-Hopton Top and Hopton Top-Longcliffe. From the top of Hopton Incline (a little under 5 miles out from High Peak Junction) the railway continued north-westwards, falling gradually on a ruling gradient of 1 in 792 towards Longcliffe. The working instructions issued by the LMSR in 1937 stipulated that: *'No train must leave Hopton Top for Longcliffe between the hours of 8.30am and 4.30pm until permission has been obtained by the guard (the driver in the case of a light engine) from Longcliffe by telephone and the driver is in possession of the staff and a ticket for the Hopton Top-Longcliffe section. Should the telephone communication have failed, necessitating a train leaving Hopton Top for Longcliffe between 8.30am and 4.30pm without permission from Longcliffe, such train must be brought to a stand at Bridge 52 (over the Brassington-Longcliffe road), about 300 yards on the Hopton side of Longcliffe Station until signalled forward by the person in charge at Longcliffe.'* On the Hopton-Longcliffe section there were three private sidings; according to the agreements in force in 1938, they were owned by: Swan Ratcliffe & Co. (Harborough brick works siding), Hopton Wood Stone firms Ltd. (Manystones siding), and Messrs. Hickman's & Co. (a stone firm - a subsidiary of Messrs. Stewarts & Lloyds).

At **Longcliffe** (2 miles from Hopton Top, 7 miles from High Peak Junction) there was a goods depot, 1,060ft above sea level, on the south side of the Ashbourne-Grangemill road (A524). It seems that the warehouse at Longcliffe was not actually provided until a few years after the railway opened, a letter from the C&HPR to a customer (Mr.Samuel Frost) dated 13 June 1834 referring to: '.....the rent

Cromford Goods Wharf, photographed from the north bank of the canal, 10 October 1951. North London Tank No.58850 shunts. PHOTOGRAPH: F.W. SHUTTLEWORTH, COURTESY INDUSTRIAL RAILWAY SOCIETY

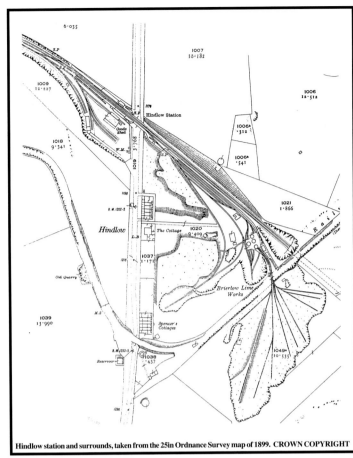

Hindlow station and surrounds, taken from the 25in Ordnance Survey map of 1899. **CROWN COPYRIGHT**

C&HPR's minute books reveals that the company had other interests at Longcliffe - it was noted on 24 November 1851 that: '.....*the Beer House at Longcliffe is let to Mr.Frost and the company receive five pounds per annum rent.*' The 'beer house' had actually first been let in 1843. Also in 1843, incidentally, the company had turned down a request to let a 'dwelling house' at Parsley Hay be used as a public house.

Continuing north-westwards from Longcliffe, the railway undulated gently across the bare hills - apart from the occasional farmhouse or quarry this section bore scant evidence of human habitation. On the east side of the line was Glossop's Siding which served Minninglow Quarry; traffic for this siding had to be attached and detached only by down trains. There were also

of the Longcliffe Wharf, with the addition of the new Warehouse recently built, will be raised to the sum of twenty five pounds per annum....' Following the alterations to parts of the route in the 1890s, Longcliffe became a staff station for the exchange of the Hopton Top-Longcliffe and the Longcliffe-Friden train staffs.

The two principal traffics at Longcliffe were coal, brought in for local residential and industrial use, and limestone, which was extracted from a local quarry. At one time there was also a siding to a fowl grit factory. A snippet in the

sidings serving Messrs. G.Lovegrove's Hoe Grange Quarry (the Longcliffe Limestone Co.), and the Sheepbridge Coal & Iron Co. - a pre-1922 plan of the latter shows an engine house alongside the siding, indicating that the siding was rope-worked.

Another feature on this section was a pair of stone-faced embankments. Constructed originally of earth, the two embankments soon required buttressing in stone - the C&HPR records show that in the early spring of 1839 2,851 square yards of land were purchased for the strengthening of the '8 mile embankment' (8 miles from Cromford

Wharf), and 2,154 square yards for the '9 mile embankment'.

At **Minninglow** (3 miles from Longcliffe, 10 miles from High Peak Junction), there was a goods depot which comprised a loading dock and a couple of sidings. At one time, one of the sidings used to serve a brick works. At the north-west end of the depot the line crossed Mouldridge Lane on the level, and given that the crossing was ungated and the approach from the west considerably obscured by trees, the working instructions required that all drivers should '.....bring their engines to a dead stand short of the crossing, and not proceed until satisfied that animals or vehicles are not about to cross the railway'.

A little to the north-west of Minninglow was **Gotham Curve** which, with a radius of only 2¹/₂ chains, was purported in BR days to be the sharpest curve on any running line in Britain. Prior to the 1950s, the curve had a superelevation of *eleven* inches. On the operating side, the tightness of Gotham Curve was the principal reason why six-wheeled vehicles (other than specially approved water tenders) were strictly prohibited south of Friden - in later years, in particular, the line's inability to accommodate larger wagons was considered to be a major obstacle to economic operations.

Northwards from Gotham, the railway crossed the Friden-Cromford road (later the A5012) on the level. This was known as Newhaven Crossing. The working instructions for 1937 stated that between 7.0am and 7.0pm '.....drivers must whistle for the gates to be opened by the gate-woman'. After 7.0pm or on Sundays, the responsibility for opening and closing the crossing gates lay with the guard of the train.

Friden (2¹/₂ miles from Minninglow and 12¹/₂ from High Peak Junction) was another staff station, the Longcliffe-Friden and Friden-Parsley Hay train staffs being exchanged there. Friden was a small goods depot comprising a loading dock, livestock pens (presumably for sheep) and a couple of sidings - one of its principal local customers was the Derbyshire Silica Fire Brick Co., adjacent to the yard and with its own siding. At one time there had been a hint that Friden might become a point of dispatch for locally extracted iron ore, a letter dated 31 October 1850 from the C&HPR to Mr.Peter Bown of Codnor Park offering: '.....*a sample of ore - the best we have seen. The party offering it has about 200 tons and he asks 9 shillings per ton delivered at Friden Wharf.*' Unfortunately, no further correspondence survives, and so we do not know if Mr.Bown took up the offer. Nevertheless, one interesting point from that brief extract is that the C&HPR was clearly not averse to acting as agent, official or otherwise, for local businessmen. We have already seen examples of the company readily recommending certain carriers, and one might ask whether 'agency' activities and recommendations were wholly ethical. Or did it help by being a C&HPR director.....?

Returning to the subject in hand, Friden was the point where BR 'main line' locomotives - usually a 3F 0-6-0 or, latterly, often an Ivatt 2MT 2-6-0 - took over from C&HPR locos. The WTT for 1957, for example, listed one 'main line' train, empties from Buxton, arriving at Friden in the morning (9.40am) and one outwards (dep.Friden for Hindlow 1.55pm SX or 12.30).

From Friden, the C&HPR continued its gradual rise and passed through the 51 yard Newhaven Tunnel underneath the main Buxton-Ashbourne road (A515) before entering **Parsley Hay sta-**

It was 1965 when a 204hp diesel shunter took over permanently on High Peak Junction - Cromford Wharf duties, but a similar lightweight diesel was photographed manoeuvring near the bottom of Cromford Incline on 13 July 1961. **PHOTOGRAPH: E.R.MORTEN**

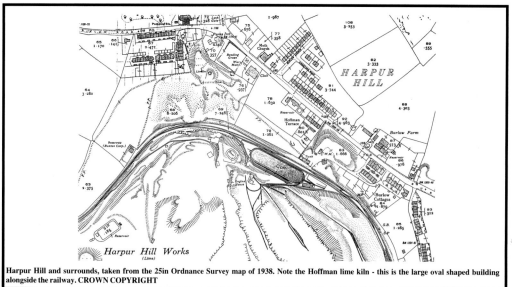

Harpur Hill and surrounds, taken from the 25in Ordnance Survey map of 1938. Note the Hoffman lime kiln - this is the large oval shaped building alongside the railway. **CROWN COPYRIGHT**

upgraded in stages between 1869 and 1892 and so we have, in effect, an 'old' and a 'new' C&HPR, albeit with some parts being common to both. Some of the alterations were simply much-needed improvements to the C&HPR itself, but others were in connection with the LNWR's new line from Buxton to Ashbourne, which was completed through to Ashbourne in August 1899. The Buxton-Hindlow-Parsley Hay section was ultimately double track throughout, and after the alterations which took place in the 1890s it was worked on the absolute block system. We shall look at the 'old' and the 'new' routes in turn, but for the sake of simplicity we shall avoid delving into every nook and cranny.....

THE 'OLD' ROUTE: One of the principal purposes of realigning the railway was to circumvent **Hurdlow Incline** - 850 yards at 1 in 16, worked by a 20hp engine. The new avoiding line was brought into use on 4 January 1869, and the incline fell into disuse. It is believed that the engine was cannibalised for spare parts. Reynolds's report of Hurdlow engine in 1852 had noted: *'Cylinders want reboring; both valve casings broken. One boiler very bad. Repair, say £270.'* From Hurdlow Top the old line continued to Dowlow, north of which was a triangle for turning wagons - as explained earlier, some wagons used on the line had end doors, and these had to be taken up and down the inclines with the doors uppermost. Beyond Dowlow the line twisted and turned ferociously to follow the contours of the land, on its way to **Harpur Hill** ($23\frac{1}{2}$ miles from High Peak Junction). The original Dowlow-Harpur Hill section was superseded by a new alignment in 1892. Between Harpur Hill and **Old Harpur** the original route incorporated numerous sharp curves, but be-

tion ($2\frac{1}{2}$ miles from Friden, 15 miles from High Peak Junction). This was a junction station - the LNWR Ashbourne branch, opened in 1899, joined the C&HPR a little to the south of the station. For its new status as a passenger station, 'proper' facilities were provided - previously, it had been one of the C&HPR's archetypally Spartan goods depots. In the C&HPR's early years the warehouse at Parsley Hay (and a nearby residential house) had been let to Mr.Nathaniel Wheatcroft. This is the C&HPR writing to Mr.N.Wheatcroft on 26 March 1838: *'.....re- the shamefully dilapidated state in which the Parsley Hay warehouse has been for a length of time.....request that it be immediately put into proper repair.'* On a different note, in 1843 the C&HPR levied a charge of 2d per ton on all articles sent to Parsley Hay 'in lieu of rent for the use of the wharf and the weighing machines'.

Parsley Hay station marked the end of the staff section from Friden. That said, in the C&HPR's last years - when railway 'souvenir hunters' were extremely active - it was usual for crews to carry the Parsley Hay-Friden and Friden-Middleton Top train staffs together on the engine. Parsley Hay station was very remote and, arguably, its principal benefit to the locals was that mobile water tanks could be stationed there - for many of the cottagers who lived in the area, these tanks were the only source of domestic water. Due to its remoteness Parsley Hay station never handled a great deal of passenger traffic, and there were few local protests when it closed to passengers on 1 November 1954 - the date on which passenger services on the Buxton-Ashbourne branch were withdrawn.

The section of the C&HPR north-west from Parsley Hay was considerably realigned and

The engine shed at Sheep Pasture Top, housing a 'Chopper' 2-4-0T, in July 1935. The building was destroyed by a gale in 1962. **PHOTOGRAPH: W.A.CAMWELL, COURTESY PETER WARD**

tween 1868 and 1875 a new, straighter alignment was built between those points.

THE 'NEW' ROUTE: Starting near the foot of the disused Hurdlow Incline, the new alignment passed through **Hurdlow Station** (2¼ miles from Parsley Hay) and then continued, on a ruling gradient of 1 in 60, to rejoined the old alignment near **Dowlow halt** (4½ miles from Parsley Hay). Dowlow halt was actually a later addition, opening as an unadvertised workmen's halt in 1920 and becoming a public halt on 4 November 1929. The halt was 1,260ft above sea level, and was the highest point on the Buxton-Ashbourne route. Near Dowlow halt were the High Peak Lime Works and **Briggs Siding**, which was brought into use circa 1907. The siding was named after its one of its original joint owners, Messrs. R.Briggs & Co., who were later taken over by the Buxton Lime firms Co. which, in turn, became part of ICI (Lime Division) Ltd. The section of line near Briggs Siding is, incidentally, still in use today - it is the only part of the C&HPR which remains operational, albeit in a much realigned and upgraded form. A little beyond Dowlow, the new alignment diverged from the old once again - it adopted an altogether straighter course than the original line, partly with the aid of the 514 yard-long **Hindlow Tunnel** under Brier Low. At the north end of the tunnel was **Hindlow Station** (5½ miles from Parsley Hay), near which were sidings to Hindlow Quarry (opened in the late 1920s) and Beswick Lime Works. A little beyond Hindlow a single track diverged from the new main line and, after running parallel with it for nearly a mile on the down side, turned away on a rising gradient of 1 in 42 to join the old C&HPR line just to the south of Harpur Hill. The new line between Hindlow and Parsley Hay - some three quarters of a mile shorter than the old alignment - was a component of the LNWR's Buxton-Ashbourne line. After the alterations which took

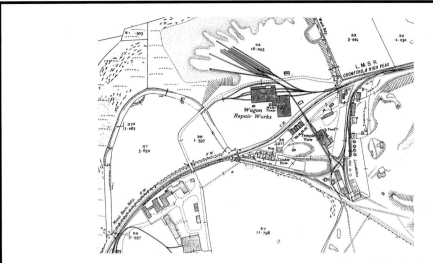

Old Harpur, 25in Ordnance Survey map of 1938. Note the original alignment of the C&HPR, still clearly defined as the 'figure of eight'. CROWN COPYRIGHT

place in the 1890s, the entire Parsley Hay-Hindlow section was worked on the absolute block system.

Resuming our journey at Old Harpur, the railway then continued to **Ladmanlow** (25 miles from High Peak Junction on the original alignment). An engine shed was provided at Ladmanlow around 1860, two locomotives being allocated there. The shed remained in use until 1892 when the Ladmanlow-Shallcross section was abandoned, and its locomotives were transferred to Buxton.

Prior to the 1890s Ladmanlow was considered, by the C&HPR and its customers, to be the best wharfing point for Buxton, being only a mile and a half from the centre of the town. On occasions, though, the C&HPR seemed to overlook that 1½-mile gap, as the company's minute books frequently refer to 'Buxton' station, when they really mean Ladmanlow.

The Harpur Hill-Ladmanlow section was the highest part of the C&HPR route - between those points the summit of 1,266ft was attained. Importantly, that section once generated a healthy

amount of traffic, there being several rail-connected industrial concerns in the area, some of them with their own private railway systems. Among the larger concerns were Grin Quarries (opened 1832, own branch line laid in 1857), the Hoffman Lime Kiln (lit in 1875 and burned continuously until 1952), Hillhead Quarries (opened 1927), and the Safety in Mines Research Centre (opened 1920s). The 1938 *Handbook of Stations*, published by the Railway Clearing House, listed Dolby's Siding, Hoffman Kiln, Crusher Siding, Chatter Siding, Old Kiln Siding, Cinder Row, and the Central Stores & Wagon Repair Workshops. All were part of ICI (Lime Division) Ltd. By the early 1950s, however, the traffic from the industries around Ladmanlow had declined, and on 2 August 1954 the railway was truncated at a point near the ICI wagon repair workshops, between Harpur Hill and Old Harpur.

Following the changes of the 1890s the Harpur Hill-Old Harpur section was worked as a goods yard, while the Old Harpur-Ladmanlow section was worked on the 'one engine in steam' principle, by train staff without tickets. By the 1960s, when only the Hindlow-Harpur Hill section remained, staff and ticket working was the order of the day.

Going back to the 1860s, shortly after the LNWR take-over of the C&HPR there were plans to transfer the engineering workshops to Ladmanlow, but those plans were not pursued - an oft-repeated reason for having the workshops remain at Cromford is that the staff there were settled, but there might have been another reason. The men employed on the High Peak line were poorly paid, even by the standards of the day, and had the LNWR moved the workshops to Ladmanlow they would probably have had to pay higher wages in order to attract staff.

As for the section of the railway north of Ladmanlow, that was closed as far as Shallcross as early as 27 June 1892. At Ladmanlow, the line was truncated just on the south side of the old Buxton-Macclesfield road, a few yards to the north of Burbage Reservoir. As explained elsewhere, the closure of the seven-mile section between Ladmanlow and Shallcross section was due to the provision of connections to the new main line between Buxton and Hindlow. For northbound traffic from the Ladmanlow area the new route via Hindlow might have been more circuitous, but it circumvented two rope-worked inclines. North of Ladmanlow, the old

A time of transition at Middleton Top - it is 1960, and the last surviving North London Tank, No.58850, stands in front of J94 0-6-0ST No.68030. PHOTOGRAPH: PETER WARD

North London Tank No.58860 (note *LMS*) approaches the stop board at the end of the Longcliffe - Friden staff section, 150yds short of Friden station. PHOTOGRAPH: W.A.CAMWELL, COURTESY PETER WARD

line passed through **Burbage Tunnel** (also referred to as Buxton Tunnel), which was originally 638 yards long but later shortened to 580 yards. The railway then rounded the appropriately named Wild Moor, and descended **Bunsall Incline**. This originally comprised two separate inclines - Bunsall Upper (660yds at 1 in 7^1/2) and Bunsall Lower (455yds at 1 in 7), each worked by a separate two-cylinder 40hp engine. In 1852 Reynolds reported on Bunsall Upper engine: *'Wants two new cylinders and covers, bottom and valve casing or nozzles. Complete air pumps and condensers supposed good, but want examining. Wants a new driving pinion, and the wheel is scarcely fit to work. Reversing gear is required for this engine. Probable cost of repairs etc - £600.'* Reynolds noted that Bunsall Lower engine was soon to become

redundant (the two inclines were combined in June 1857), and suggested that the wheel from one of its engines could be used at Bunsall Upper. Similar to the combining of Cromford and Sheep Pasture Inclines, the combining of the two Bunsall inclines had been made possible partly by the availability of comparatively lightweight hemp ropes to replace the heavy chains. Nevertheless, in 1862 the hemp rope at Bunsall was replaced by a wire rope. Bunsall Incline became redundant in June 1892 when the entire section between Ladmanlow and Shallcross Foot was closed.

Continuing northwards from Bunsall the railway stuck very close to the 750ft contour line on the east side of the picturesque Goyt Valley - this part of the valley now accommodates Fernilee Reservoir, which was formally opened in June 1937.

From what is now the northern end of the reservoir, the railway continued almost due north to the head of **Shallcross Incline**, 817 yards at 1 in 10ˇ, and worked by a 40hp engine. It was the last of the inclines to convert from chains to a hemp rope (in May 1865), and the last to switch from a hemp to a wire rope (in February 1868). After this engine became redundant in 1892, parts were subsequently incorporated in the Middleton engine.

It is believed that there was once an engine shed at Shallcross Top - presumably, it was provided when locomotive working between Shallcross and Bunsall Foot commenced in the early 1860s. Whatever its origins, it would obviously have become redundant in 1892. Near Shallcross Foot, a siding was installed at Fernilee in 1860 for Messrs.Ellam and Jones for their barytes traffic, which was said to be bound for 'London and other places'.

The closures of 1892 affected the railway only as far as the foot of Shallcross Incline. From that point, the remaining mile or so of line to Whaley Bridge was kept open - right through until 30 January 1965, in fact - in order to serve the gas works at Shallcross Foot (originally the Chapel, Whaley & District Gas Co.). From Shallcross Foot, the C&HPR passed under a low bridge beneath the LNWR Stockport-Buxton main line near Whaley Bridge station. It is known that the C&HPR's two Vulcan Foundry locomotives of 1860 were built to a restricted height, supposedly for working under this particular bridge, although there is some considerable doubt if they were actually used at Whaley Bridge at all. Furthermore, those two locomotives had both been withdrawn by 1880 and there is no evidence to sug-

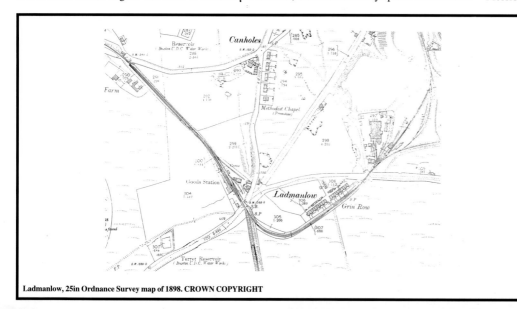

Ladmanlow, 25in Ordnance Survey map of 1898. CROWN COPYRIGHT

J94 No.68006, with water tanks in tow - period believed to be March 1966. The location is Newhaven Crossing, which took the C&HPR across the Cromford - Newhaven road (A5012), and this raises a query - the train seems to be heading south, but as the leading tender is six-wheeled (not to mention comparatively modern and possibly in revenue earning service), where could it have been going? PHOTOGRAPH: ANDREW MUCKLEY

gest that they were replaced by others. Nevertheless, locomotives certainly *could* penetrate Shallcross Yard from a different direction - this was by means of the connecting line which had been installed in 1857 between the C&HPR and the main line a little to the south of Whaley Bridge station.

After passing under the low bridge beneath the main line, the C&HPR negotiated **Whaley Bridge Incline**, the last major obstacle on its route. The incline, which was 180 yards long and graded at 1 in 13, took the railway down to a basin on the Peak Forest Canal. It is clear that the incline was initially horse-worked, a letter from John Leonard (the C&HPR's general manager) to Mr.Meadows, of the Peak Forest Canal Co., on 15 August 1833 opining that: '.....*the Engine at the Whaley inclined plane should be immediately erected and set to work, but in order to do this it will be first necessary to have a supply of water for it. It has been suggested that water might be had for this purpose from the feeder of the Peak Forest Canal, but I am not aware that permission has ever been obtained to do so, or that application has been made for such permission.....You are no doubt sufficiently acquainted with the properties of the Steam Engine to know that the water required for their use is not wasted, at least not so as to be perceptible, so that in requesting to be allowed to take the water from the feeder we are simply asking permission to intercept a part and make use of it in working the Steam Engine previous to it being applied to the use of the Canal.'*

The incline was initially worked, wherever possible, by balancing ascending and descending loads, but if no balancing load were available horses were used. It appears that the winding engine - a two-cylinder unit rated at 10hp - was finally brought into use until 1838, but it didn't have a particularly long life, being disabled by mining subsidence underneath the incline. In 1862 the engine was reported to be out of use, but it was decided not to rebuild it and, instead, to revert to counterbalance and horse operation. Matters were improved very slightly around 1890 when a horse-operated capstan was installed at the top of the incline. This mode of working continued until the closure of the incline in 1952.

A short distance beyond the foot of the incline was the **Peak Forest Canal Basin** (33 and three quarters of a mile from High Peak Junction), which was the C&HPR's northern extremity and the point where railway/canal traffic was exchanged - remember that, prior to 1857, the canal was the only means of transportation for goods between Whaley Bridge and Manchester. Whaley Bridge, incidentally, was 517ft above sea level, and the C&HPR's descent from Bunsall Top had involved a drop of 700ft in about 4 1/2 miles.

The familiar landmark of the Hoffman limekiln chimney near Harpur Hill, 10 September 1950. The kiln was first lit in 1875, and burned continuously until its closure in 1952. PHOTOGRAPH: E.R.MORTEN

Following the closure of the Ladmanlow - Shallcross section in 1892, Ladmanlow became the northern terminus of the C&HPR. The line actually terminated about half a mile north of Ladmanlow Goods Station - that station is seen here, with 3F 0-6-0 No.43268 shunting on 20 June 1951. The level crossing in the distance carried the railway over the Buxton-Leek (A53) road, about 1° miles from the centre of Buxton. PHOTOGRAPH: E.R.MORTEN

Shallcross Yard remained open until 1965, partly to serve the gas works. This picture, taken on 10 September 1950, looks south towards the foot of the disused Shallcross Incline. PHOTOGRAPH: E.R.MORTEN

Rails

In case it needs to be emphasised, the C&HPR was a standard gauge concern. The original rails were of the fish-belly type - they were cast iron, 4ft long, weighed 84lb each (63lb/yd), and were laid on stone blocks. Some of these rails were still *in situ* in the workshop at Cromford at the time of the railway's demise in 1967, after a working life of 137 years. From the mid-1840s, wrought iron bridge rails weighing 45lb/yd and timber sleepers (initially longitudinal ones) started to replace the original fish-belly rails and stone blocks on parts of the 'main line'.

When extensive improvements to the line were being considered in 1855/56, one item under regular discussion was the switch to locomotive haulage. With the use of locomotives in mind the C&HPR extended feelers for sources of second-hand wrought iron rails, and it was confirmed that suitable rails were available from, amongst others, the GWR, the Midland Railway, and an unspecified source in Ireland. It is, however, uncertain whether rails were actually obtained from any of those sources, as the C&HPR's abysmal financial state frequently resulted in proposals and recommendations being shelved. That said, in January 1860 the company opened negotiations for seventy tons of wrought iron rails (weighing 50lb/yd) for relaying the Sheep Pasture Top-Middleton Bottom section in anticipation of a significant increase in traffic from the local quarries.

Following the LNWR 'take over' of the C&HPR in 1861 the new proprietors gradually relayed the line with second-hand wrought iron rails laid on transverse sleepers, but it was 1867 before cast iron rails and stone blocks had been replaced on the whole of the 'main line'. As far as can be determined, the next major bout of relaying took place in 1925, with 'serviceable' LNWR rails being used. It was noted that these rails were in 30ft lengths - they had originally weighed 90lb/yd but by the mid-1930s were reckoned to be 81lb. The usual practice at that time was for the use of 12 sleepers per rail length.

Distances

In 1892, following the opening of the Buxton-Parsley Hay line and the closure of the Ladmanlow-Shallcross Foot section of the C&HPR, the method of measuring the High Peak line was altered. Previously, 'zero' had been at Cromford (working north-westwards), but under the new method 'zero' was at Buxton (working south-eastwards). The original distances from Cromford have been quoted in the text - the revised distances from Buxton, taking into account realignments, which in some cases shortened the route, were:

Buxton	0m 0yd
Parsley Hay	9m 1109yd
Friden	12m 175yd
Minninglow	15m 89yd
Longcliffe	17m 734yd
Steeplehouse	21m 1529yd
Cromford Wharf	23m 1255yds
High Peak Jctn.	24m 39yd

The C&HPR passed under the LNWR at Whaley Bridge by means of a low bridge. Its height effectively ruled out the use of locomotives at this end of the line, although there are suggestions that 'reduced height' locomotives were actually used in the 1860s. The line on the extreme left connected the C&HPR to the LNWR. Whaley Bridge 'main line' station. PHOTOGRAPH: E.R.MORTEN

3....Locomotives

The nature of the C&HPR, especially south of Friden, placed restrictions on the types of locomotives which could be used, and after the 1930s only four types were in regular use on the southern section of the line. One of these was the ex-LNWR 'Choppers', the last survivor, as BR No.58092, seeing out its days on the line. In one of its earlier guises, No.58092 had worn LMSR No.6428, and it was photographed as such at Sheep Pasture Top in 1935. PHOTOGRAPH: E.R.MORTEN

'....my intention, when the locomotive engines were first made, was to recommend the Company to do the haulage at $^1/_2$d per ton per mile.....'.

It has been said before, and often, but the subject of early C&HPR locomotives is extremely confused. Primary source references are sparse, and the scant details that are available often seem to be absurdly contradictory. The dearth of information is probably partly attributable to the fact that, prior to 1855, the C&HPR was not a carrier (goods were carried on the line by private traders or contractors) and so, in theory, the company would have had no use for locomotives. However, there are positive references to confirm that locomotives *were* used before 1855. Hazarding a guess, could it be that any locomotives used prior to 1855 were actually the property of individual directors or private traders, or were on trial - i.e. they were *not* actually owned by the C&HPR itself? Please bear in mind those cautionary notes.

Early Days

When the initial survey for the railway was presented in 1824 the use of locomotives on the level sections was certainly considered, but when the line opened in 1830/31 the level sections were worked exclusively by horses. The first definite mention of the use of locomotives was in December 1834, when the *Derby Mercury* referred to a locomotive being assembled - presumably from ready made parts - at the Cromford workshop. In June 1835 the same newspaper carried a report of a locomotive being tried near Middleton Top. There is no mention of either event in the C&HPR's own records, but if such an omission seems rather curious please bear in mind the earlier comments above..........

As for the identities of the two locomotives featured in the newspaper reports, it has of-

ten been suggested that the C&HPR's first locomotives were a Robert Stephenson 0-4-0 of 1833 and an Edward Bury 2-2-0 of 1835, both possibly acquired second-hand. Frustratingly, though, there is nothing conclusive to tie either locomotive to either of the newspaper accounts.

There is evidence to suggest that one, or probably two, locomotives were assembled at the workshops at Cromford under the direction of the company's general manager and engineer, John Leonard. Whatever the genesis of the locomotives, the fact that there were two in action on the

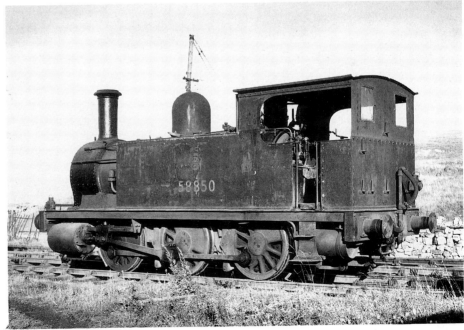

C&HPR by the mid-1840s seems to be supported by Leonard's reference, on 25 February 1845, to: '....my intention, when the locomotive engines (*plural*) were first made, was to recommend the Company to do the haulage at $^1/_2$d per ton per mile.....'. The company records make no further reference to these two locomotives.

When the C&HPR was reincorporated in 1855 it was authorised to become a carrier, and so the subject of locomotive traction was placed high on the list of priorities. Captain Moorsom's report of 8 August 1855 referred to '.....the provi-

The last of the class - North London Tank No.58850 at Middleton Top in 1960. PHOTOGRAPH: PETER WARD

Three Kitson/BR 0F 0-4-0STs worked on the C&HPR, the longest resident of that trio being No.47000. In July 1955 that engine suffered the ignominy of a derailment at Steeplehouse, due to vandalism, and after being rerailed had to be taken to Derby for repairs. It returned to the C&HPR on 24 October, coming in via Parsley Hay and Middleton Incline. Here, the rope is being attached to the returning loco at Middleton Top. PHOTOGRAPH: E.R.MORTEN

sion of locomotives and their stables', and to offers from 'good makers' to supply two locomotives and tenders for £2,000. Significantly, the wording of Moorsom's report implied that, at that time, there were *no* locomotives in use on the line - presumably the earlier locomotives had already been dispensed with. By 30 January 1856 the position had changed, the directors noting that '.....a locomotive engine now runs from the top of the Buxton (Bunsall) incline to the Hurdlow incline, a distance of about twelve miles, and another will shortly be at work'. The second engine was delivered in February, but at the end of that month it was reported as being: '.....under alteration with a view of making it better suited to the cast iron rails, but it is doubtful whether the proposed alteration will entirely obviate the present operation arising from its excessive weight'. This sounds like a second-hand locomotive, as an excessively heavy machine would, presumably, not have been ordered new.

In 1857 the C&HPR was in need of additional locomotive power, and so the directors authorised the purchase of an engine '.....for an amount not exceeding £500'. The engine in question was stated to be '.....now on the Eastern Counties Line.....'. Details of this engine are uncertain (and it is unconfirmed whether the C&HPR actually made the purchase), but there is a possibility that it might have been a contractor's engine.

Despite the foregoing, by September 1858 there were *no* locomotives working on the C&HPR - a minute from the directors' meeting on 10 September noted that: '.....a great advantage would result to the company were the line worked by Locomotive power instead of horse power as at present.....' At that same meeting, the directors conceded that the company was not in a financial position to purchase locomotives, but it was proposed that a private company be formed to buy locomotives which could be rented to the C&HPR. It is unclear whether the proposed 'leasing' com-

pany was established, although on 1 October 1858 - i.e. just three weeks after the proposal was made - it was noted that the directors were: '.....about to arrange for the hire of Locomotive Engines to work the line between Hopton and Ladmanlow.'

Somewhat more definite is the fact that, immediately prior to the commencement of the LNWR's lease in 1861, the C&HPR had seven locomotives. That said, there is considerable vagueness about what they were and where they had come from, and one might also ask whether the alleged numbers (of the early locomotives, at least) were anything more than book entries. The following

list of C&HPR locomotives is based loosely on an extensive article which appeared in the *SLS Journal* of August 1951:

'**No.1**': Thought to be the Stephenson 0-4-0 of 1833 (Works No.45), possibly purchased second-hand. Length 14ft, weight 7 tons, wheels 5ft diameter, cylinders 12in.x16in.. Possibly named PEAK. Repaired twice by the LNWR in 1861. Was put to use as a stationary engine at the Cromford workshops in May 1863. Disposed of before 1871.

'**No.2**': Believed to be a 2-2-0 built by Edward Bury in 1835 (Works No.22), probably acquired second-hand. Length (engine only) 18ft

While No.47000 was sidelined due to its derailment, ex-Midland 0-4-0T No.41536 was immediately drafted in as a temporary replacement. One of the incomer's first tasks was to assist, on 1 August 1955, in the re-railing of No.47000. PHOTOGRAPH: E.R.MORTEN

Former Caledonian Railway 0-4-0ST No.56020 was, perhaps, an unlikely incomer to the C&HPR, but it actually had two periods on the line, one at the end of 1948 and the other in the Summer of 1952. This is the latter occasion, the location being Cromford Wharf. PHOTOGRAPH: DEREK CLAYTON

6in, weight 9½ tons, driving wheels 4ft 8in, cylinders 12in.x18in.. Reputedly named LIVERPOOL. Became **LNWR No.2039** in 1871, later duplicated as **No.1942**. Rebuilt as a saddle tank and transferred to the Locomotive Machinery Department for shunting duties at Crewe Works. Scrapped May 1876.

'No.3': Possibly a Neilson 0-6-0ST. Might this have been the Eastern Counties engine, referred to above? One alternative theory is that it was named BURY and was a sister engine of 2-2-0 'No.2' LIVERPOOL, while another theory is that it was built (assembled?) by the C&HPR, possibly at Cromford. Whatever the case, there is no record of this locomotive working between 1860 and 1871. It was definitely withdrawn by the latter date.

No.4: An 0-6-0ST, usually acknowledged as being built at the Cromford workshop in 1859. It has, however, been suggested that it was originally one of the Cromford-built engines of the early 1840s, being *rebuilt* in 1859. Length 21ft, weight 12¾ tons, wheels 3ft 0in, cylinders 10in.x12in.. Worked mainly on the Sheep Pasture Top-Middleton Foot section. Became **LNWR No.2040**, later duplicated as **No.1943**. Transferred to Loco Machinery Dept; withdrawn 1882.

No.5: Sister engine to No.4, commenced work in January 1860. In its later years worked mainly at Cromford. Became **LNWR No.2041**, then duplicated as **No.1944**. Transferred to Loco Machinery Dept; disposal unknown.

No.6: Vulcan Foundry 0-6-0ST (Works No.435), built 1860. Length 21ft 8in, weight 14tons 9cwt, wheels 3ft 0in, cylinders 9in.x15in., boiler pressure 100lb. Built to loading gauge of only 9ft 10½in allegedly for duties on restricted-height line under LNWR at Whaley Bridge, but it appears that it was used almost exclusively south of Ladmanlow. Became **LNWR No.2042**, then duplicated as **No.1945**. Withdrawn 1879.

No.7: Similar to No.6. (Vulcan Works No.436). Again, despite being built to a low loading

gauge (allegedly for duties at Whaley Bridge), it seems to have spent its life working southwards from Ladmanlow. Became **LNWR No.2043**, then duplicated as **No.1946**. Transferred to Loco Machinery Dept. Sold for £225 in 1880.

Distribution
Before proceeding with details of how locomotive matters changed under LNWR management, it should be emphasised once again that the nature of the line required specialised working practices - it wasn't simply a case of hitching up wagons to a locomotive at one end and having the loco haul the wagons right through to the other end. The fact that the line was punctuated by rope-worked inclines meant that each 'level' section between inclines was worked, in effect, as a separate entity. For this, a locomotive (or two) was allotted to each 'level', and worked only between the top of one incline and the foot of the next. That said, engines obviously had to go away for repairs from time to time, and when this was required they were taken down the inclines, as necessary, in steam *and* on the rope. As can be imagined, the passage of a locomotive up or down an incline was somewhat tedious, and was therefore undertaken only when necessary. Consequently, once a locomotive was ensconced on a particular level, it tended to remain there unless a move became essential.

By the early 1860s locomotives were in use on all the levels except Whaley Bridge-Shallcross Bottom and Middleton Top-Hopton Bottom. That latter exception continued until April 1877 when Hopton Incline was remodelled specifically with locomotive working in mind. Subsequently, the entire section between Middleton Top and Bunsall Top was worked as one.

The First Incomers
Starting in June 1861, the LNWR started to draft in its own engines to the C&HPR. At that time, two or three were normally used simultaneously on the line, but by the late 1860s six or more were

usually in action at any one time. Many of the incomers were decidedly non-standard absorbed engines, but from October 1863 Alexander Allan's 'Crewe Goods' - either in their original 2-4-0 format or after rebuilding as 2-4-0Ts - started a gradual take-over. During the late 1890s the 'Crewe Goods' usually worked the milk traffic off the C&HP to Buxton, and one of the class, No.3022, was still a Buxton engine at the time of its withdrawal in June 1904. During the late 1890s it had helped out on contractor's duties on the new Ashbourne line, and had latterly been the spare C&HP engine.

One distinctive incomer - albeit not in a revenue earning capacity - was the experimental 'Fell' locomotive which, by using a system of levers and bevel wheels to 'grip' a specially-installed centre rail, could work on very steep gradients. The prototype engine undertook a series of public demonstrations on the C&HP - believed to be on the Whaley Bridge-Shallcross section - in 1863/64. Another demonstration took place in 1876, this time with a locomotive fitted with 'Handyside Steep Gradient' equipment which was put to the test on Hopton Incline.

The Bissel Tanks
Francis Webb's 0-4-2Ts of 1896-1901 were invariably known as 'Bissel Tanks' on account of their solid trailing wheels carried in a Bissel truck. The class was first tried on the C&HP in late 1890s, but their water capacities were deemed inadequate and so they were replaced by Webb 2-4-0Ts - the 'Choppers'. However, by the late 1920s five of the ten 'Choppers' had been withdrawn, and this brought about the reappearance of 'Bissel Tanks' on the C&HPR, at least five of the type being noted on the line between the late 1920s and the early 1940s. By this time the water supplies along the line had been improved and so the engines' limited capacities were less of a problem. Nevertheless, they tended to be used principally on the Cromford Wharf-High Peak Junction and the Sheep Pasture Top-Middleton Bottom sections. On the odd occa-

Ex-LMSR 350hp diesel No.12006 was tried on the C&HPR on 7 April 1959, but was found lacking. It was photographed at Parsley Hay with a BR inspector on board (well, almost!). The goods yard beyond the station, incidentally, is on the original C&HPR alignment. PHOTOGRAPH: E.R.MORTEN

sions when the 'Bissels' were used above Middleton Top, they could not work the daily milk trains to/from Longcliffe on account of having no vacuum brakes.

'The Choppers'

The origin of this sobriquet has been variously ascribed, but for the sake of this modest little book the term is used to describe Webb's 2-4-0Ts of 1876-1880, forty of which were withdrawn in the late 1890s and renewed as 2-4-2Ts. Only ten 2-4-0Ts survived, and it appears that most, if not all, of these ten worked on the C&HPR at some time or other. In 1908 five Webb 2-4-2Ts were cut down to 2-4-0Ts, but it seems that none of these five - later LMSR Nos.6430-6434 - were used on the C&HPR.

Nine of the ten 'Choppers' were withdrawn between 1924 and 1936, but the tenth, as LMSR No.6428, later No.26428, and ultimately BR No.58092, survived until March 1952. On the C&HPR, the 'Choppers' didn't usually work above Middleton in their later years, and the last survivor, No.58092, was no exception, spending its final years on the Sheep Pasture Top-Middleton Bottom section.

The North London Tanks

In 1931 the first of the ex-North London Railway 0-6-0Ts appeared on the C&HPR, establishing a presence which was to last for almost thirty years. Ten of the NLR tanks are known to have worked on the line at various times, and four were still there in the BR era. These were Nos.58850, 58856, 58860 and 58862. The last to survive was No.58850, which saw out its days on the C&HPR - it is believed to have performed its last revenue earning tasks early in 1960, subsequently being placed in store at Middleton Top before being dispatched to Rowsley shed in the summer. It was withdrawn from Rowsley in September 1960, but was later acquired for preservation and now lives on the Bluebell Railway.

Inevitably, visits to the line were reported in the contemporary railway press, and the distribution of the NLR tanks was duly noted:
Sunday 12.12.1948: Nos.58856 and 58862 were at Middleton Top; No.27505 (yet to receive its BR number, 58850) was at Rowsley for a washout. (The fourth of the regular quartet, No.58860, was under repair at Bow Works).
Sunday 17.7.1949: No.58856 at Middleton Top; No.58850 at Cromford; No.58860 at Rowsley.
Tuesday 10.4.1956: Nos.58850 and 58856 working Middleton Top-Friden; No.58860 at the parent shed at Rowsley; (No.58862 had been withdrawn the previous month).
Wednesday 13.11.1957: No.58850 (by then the only survivor) shunting at Cromford.
1959 - various dates: No.58850 working Middleton Top-Friden.

Kitson/BR 0-4-0STs

The LMSR Kitson-built 0-4-0STs made their debut on the C&HP before the war. No.7000 (as it then was) was transferred to the parent shed at Rowsley as early as 1938, and although transferred to other duties in 1942 it returned (as BR No.47000) to the C&HP in 1952, and was used, most frequently, on the Sheep Pasture Top-Middleton Bottom section. During its absence in 1955 (for repairs after its derailment at Steeplehouse) ex-Midland 0-4-0T No.41536 deputised, and had stints at the Cromford Wharf end of the line and also at Sheep Pasture Top.

One of the BR-built versions of the Kitson 0-4-0STs, No.47007, also worked on the C&HP, being transferred to Rowsley (for outstationing on the C&HPR) in January 1959 - for most of the time it worked the Sheep Pasture Top-Middleton Bottom section. Another member of the class, No.47006, was transferred to Rowsley in November 1963 - it was normally stationed at Sheep Pasture Top principally for working the Hopton Wood Quarry branch (7.15am to 4.30pm as required). On 2 November 1965 No.47000 took

over from No.47006 at Sheep Pasture Top, the latter being placed in store at Cromford, nominally as a spare for its fellow.

On 26 September 1966, following the introduction of a 204hp diesel shunter (D2383) on the Sheep Pasture Top-Middleton Bottom section, principally for Middleton Quarry traffic, No.47000 was brought down Sheep Pasture Incline. This was almost certainly the last time a steam engine negotiated the incline. As far as can be determined none of the three Kitson/BR 0-4-0STs used on the C&HPR had ever worked above Middleton - at least, not in a revenue earning capacity.

Mention has been made of the parent shed at Rowsley. A brief word of explanation is in order....... Until 1935 the three C&HPR sheds had been under the control of the ex-LNWR shed at Buxton, but despite their transfer to the jurisdiction of Rowsley (an ex-Midland depot), Buxton continued to supply the engine for Middleton Top. This remained so until the early 1950s when Middleton Top once again became a sub of Rowsley - thus all three C&HPR sheds once again paid allegiance to Rowsley (17D - recoded 17C in April 1958). That said, Rowsley shed actually saw very little of its nominal siblings, the regular C&HPR locos usually remaining at their respective sub-sheds. There were further changes to the 'parent shed' situation in the 1960s, more of which anon.

Other Types

Although the North London Tanks were closely associated with the C&HPR during the BR era, they did not have a monopoly. Among the other types seen on the line was ex-Midland 0-4-0ST No.41518, which was tried - seemingly with little success - at Cromford in late 1948. One of the more unusual incomers was ex-Caledonian 0-4-0ST No.56020 which, in late 1948 and again in the summer of 1952, deputised on shunting duties at Cromford while the regular locomotive was under repair. The Caley engine was itself relieved at

J94 No.68006 was transferred to the C&HPR in 1956, and was still there at the end, eleven years later. This is Hopton Incline on 17 July 1963, the train probably having been divided for the ascent. PHOTOGRAPH: R.M. CASSERLEY COLLECTION

Cromford in July 1952 by ex-Lancashire & Yorkshire 0-4-0ST No.51235 - one of a class which, seemingly, penetrated almost everywhere! As mentioned earlier, ex-Midland 0-4-0T No.41536 had a brief stint on the line in 1955.

The J94 0-6-0STs

During the C&HPR's later years, the J94 'Austerity' 0-6-0STs forged a strong association with the line. The first J94 to arrive was No.68030, formerly of Bidston, which on 10 April 1956 underwent trials, with particular attention given to its performance on Hopton Incline. It had been considered that the 11ft wheelbase, respectable tractive effort, rugged simplicity and relative modernity would make them ideal replacements for the veteran North London Tanks, but during the initial trials of No.68030 its comparatively high centre of gravity effectively prevented it from raising enough speed around the bend on the approach to Hopton Incline.

The possible problems with the J94s were evidently soon resolved, as in August 1956 not only was No.68030 officially transferred to the parent shed at Rowsley, but 68006 and 68013 were also similarly transferred. By the following month, Nos.68013 and 68030 were in regular action between Middleton Top and Friden. Other J94s subsequently came to Rowsley - No.68034 in August 1957, No.68012 in September 1959 (it was transferred away in September 1960 but returned in April 1962 as a replacement for the withdrawn No.68030), No.68079 in July 1962, and 68068 in August 1962.

A possible threat to the J94s' growing hegemony came on 7 April 1959, when ex-LMSR 350hp diesel 0-6-0 No.12006 underwent trials on the Parsley Hay-Middleton Top section. The locomotive did not fare too well - its passage over the 55-yard radius Gotham Curve was very uneasy, and it struggled to climb Hopton Incline, even without the encumbrance of a train. Apart from trials such as this, or special d.m.u. workings, the section above Middleton Top was to remain exclusively steam-worked until the very end.

Reverting briefly to the subject of engine sheds, in April 1964 Rowsley (latterly 16J) closed, and the three C&HPR subs were transferred

to the control of Derby (by then coded 16C). The High Peak engines affected were 0-4-0ST No.47006 and J94s Nos.68006, 68012, 68013, 68068 and 68079. One month later - June 1964 - the sub-shed at Middleton Top was transferred to the control of Buxton. Given that the closure of Middleton Incline had completely severed the Middleton-Friden section from the southern end of the C&HPR, it made sense for the Middleton engines to be supplied, once again, by Buxton. Accordingly, J94s Nos.68012 and 68079 were transferred from Derby to Buxton.

As from 26 April 1965 the working of the southern end of the C&HPR - between Cromford Wharf and Whatstandwell Junction - was given over to a Derby-based 204hp diesel shunter, which also shunted at Cromford Wharf. The diesel was supplied by Derby shed and changed as necessary. The diesel take-over at Cromford displaced two J94s, Nos.68006 and 68068 - these were subsequently transferred to Buxton (then coded 9L)

and placed in store as spares for Nos.68012 and 68079, the allotted Middleton Top-Friden locos. That said, usually only one of those two (more commonly No.68012) was actually out-stationed at Middleton at any given time, with the other kept as a spare.

During the last week of August 1966 350hp diesel D3778 underwent tests between Middleton Top and Friden, and it is assumed that the trials were considered satisfactory, as the locomotive was subsequently rostered to take over from the J94s on that section as from 31 August. However, for reasons that are unclear, this did not happen. By January the following year No.68006 was in regular action on the Middleton Top-Friden section, the erstwhile regular engine, No.68012, being sidelined at Buxton shed awaiting attention.

At the end of April 1967 the remaining sections of the C&HPR closed. On Sunday 30 April three enthusiasts' specials were run, with the two surviving J94s, Nos.68006 and 68012, doing the honours. On 2 May the rest of the water tanks and stock were removed from the line, and this is believed to have been the very last working, other than for track lifting purposes, on the C&HPR. Unfortunately, the identity of the locomotive which took out the empties on 2 May is unknown, although it would presumably have been one of the J94s. As for the two now-redundant locomotives, Nos.68006 and 68012, the former was soon withdrawn but the latter - by then the only survivor of its class in BR use - saw a few months more work at Westhouses shed, at Williamthorpe Colliery.

To round off the picture, contemporary reports of the allocation of the J94s on the C&HPR were:

Sunday 30.7.61: 68006 at Middleton Top, 68030 at Cromford.
Sunday 9.9.62: 68006 at Middleton Top, 68013 at Cromford.
Wednesday 3.2.65: 68079 at Middleton Top, 68068 at Cromford.
Thursday 18.2.65: 68079 at Middleton Top, 68068 at Cromford.
Monday 26.4.65: 68012 at Middleton Top.
Wednesday 1.9.65: 68012 at Middleton Top.
Saturday 18.9.65: 68012 at Middleton Top.

Middleton Top, 12 July 1966. No.68012 emerges from the shed. PHOTOGRAPH: IVO PETERS

4....Traffic

'I am desirous at all times to accommodate everyone as far as we have the means, but I cannot permit the company to be made fools of.....'

Passenger Traffic

Although the C&HPR is usually remembered today as a mineral railway, it should not be forgotten that a basic passenger service operated on the line for over forty - and possibly up to sixty or so - years. Unfortunately, the precise nature of the services - especially in the early years - is a little hazy, as very few substantiated details have survived. The sparseness of details is almost certainly due to the fact that, until 1855, the passenger services, in common with the goods workings, were *not* operated by the C&HPR itself. From the time of their introduction in June 1833 the passenger services - worked, it would appear, by just one carriage - were operated by contractors, in this case Messrs. G.Wheatcroft & Sons.

Various members of the Wheatcroft family, incidentally, had a range of business interests in the area - one of the family was a public carrier, another owned quarries at Middleton, one was a director of the C&HPR, another was later the company auditor, and it goes on...... But despite the family's close links with the C&HPR, they were not always above reproach - the company's correspondence reveals that in December 1835 Messrs. G.Wheatcroft & Sons were warned about occupying a section of Cromford Wharf which had been allotted to another trader, and in 1839 William Wheatcroft was warned about letting his staff extract limestone from the 'wrong side of the fence' (i.e. from railway land) at Middleton Incline.

Reverting to the subject in hand, one aspect of the C&HPR's reincorporation in June 1855 was that the company was empowered to '.....become carriers of passengers and goods.....', and it took over the working of the passenger service from the contractors. It seems, however, that it

initially ran seasonally, a minute of the C&HPR's directors' meeting of 30 January 1856 noting that: *'.....the carriage which ran between Cromford and Whaley last summer was productive of much convenience to the district, and of some profit to the company; it is intended to put it on the line again.'* At that same meeting, the directors reported that they: *'......do not intend to make much preparation for the passenger traffic until the Stockport & Disley (Stockport-Whaley Bridge) line be opened.'*

That last remark suggests that the C&HPR might have been planning a more comprehensive passenger service when the Stockport-Whaley Bridge main line was opened, but if that was the case the 'comprehensive' service certainly did not materialise.

Whatever the case, that report clearly confirms that the passenger service was then operated by the C&HPR itself. Further confirmation, if any were needed, was provided at the next directors' meeting on 27 February, when the passenger

The foot of Middleton incline on 4 May 1934 - the incline itself can be seen heading up through the trees on the right. The rake of wagons on the left are on the siding leading to Middlepeak Goods Depot, which served, among other things, some of the local quarries. Ample evidence of quarrying can be seen in the hillside above and behind the wagons - to the left, out of frame, are Middle Peak Quarries, which were being worked by the early 1840s, if not earlier. Behind the photographer's left shoulder was the steep incline built to connect the Midland Railway's Wirksworth branch to the C&HPR. As things turned out, the incline was never actually used for traffic. PHOTOGRAPH: H.C.CASSERLEY

'Chopper' No.58092 heads east past Black Rock *en route* for Sheep Pasture Top. As far as can be determined, all the wagons are empty. PHOTOGRAPH: R.M.CASSERLEY COLLECTION

carriage was included in an formal inventory of the C&HPR's rolling stock.

As for the passenger carriage itself, it was described in a contemporary report as having accommodation for '.....about sixteen passengers inside and fourteen outside, and being drawn by one horse.....'. The prescribed fares were 2d per mile first class, 1¹/2d second class, and 1d third class, but it is unclear whether facilities for three classes of passengers were actually provided in such a small carriage. The original vehicle was replaced in 1857 or 1858, by a vehicle best described as a brake van with auxiliary passenger accommodation - this vehicle was referred to locally as the 'fly'. A second 'fly' was subsequently provided. This, presumably, enabled the operation of a passenger service over

the entire length of the line, in *both* directions, each day - a one-way journey could take around eight hours, and so it was not possible for one 'fly' to complete a round trip in one working day. The two vehicles were replaced by the LNWR in 1873, with a pair of 'passenger guards break vans' converted from redundant LNWR vans. By this time the public use of the passenger services was very sparse, virtually all of the passengers being workmen, particularly men employed by the Buxton Lime Co. (Figures for 1861 show that 121 passengers used the line in the course of the entire year, yielding receipts of just £8).

There are several published accounts of passenger journeys on the C&HPR, but in most instances the trips seem to have been laid on spe-

cially and, consequently, have had a vague whiff of efficiency - conventionality, some might say - possibly as some sort of public relations exercise. Perhaps the only account which conveys the leisurely - and extremely unconventional - nature of everyday life was the one by Rev. F.S.Williams in his book *Our Iron Roads* (Bemrose & Son, 1883), in which he described a colleague's journey on the line: '.....I enquired of a man in the office for the train. "Do you mean the 'fly'?", was the reply. "Yes". But the official not knowing whether the 'fly' had passed or not, went out to enquire, and brought back word that it had gone, but that if I followed it up the line, I might catch it at the siding; and if not, I should be sure to overtake it at 'Middleton Run'. I accordingly gave chase, and at length caught sight of it being drawn up the incline by a rope and a stationary engine. A man at the bottom inquired if I wished to catch the 'fly', and added, "I will stop it for you at the top", which he did by a signal. A quarter of a mile ahead I joined it. (Passengers were not officially allowed to travel up or down the inclines in the carriage, but unofficial journeys certainly weren't unknown). The vehicle in which we sat was like an old omnibus. The guard stood in the middle and worked the brake through a hole in the floor.....When reaching the summit (of an unspecified incline) the guard remarked: "We may have to wait at the top". "How long?", I inquired. "Oh, it may be five minutes", he replied, "or a few hours. It all depends upon when the engine comes to take us on. Yesterday", he added, "it did not come at all". To while away the time I walked along the line, and my fellow passengers went mushrooming. In about three hours an engine came from Whaley Bridge to fetch us, and after the driver, fireman and guard had refreshed themselves at a little public house not far away, and had freely commented on their 'horse', they went back along the line, brought up the 'fly', and having refreshed themselves again, we started..... We reached Park Gates, about a mile*

During the C&HPR's later years, in particular, its unsuitability for large, modern mineral wagons was a significant handicap. Because of the curves and the loading gauge, only relatively small (or obsolete) wagons could be used, and this was considered uneconomical. On 18 June 1965, J94 No.68012 approaches Hopton Summit with mineral wagons from Prestwich Intake Quarry - the wagon seen here was the largest type to be used on the C&HPR. PHOTOGRAPH: DEREK CROSS

from Buxton, at seven o'clock, after a journey of about twenty miles, in six hours'.

The somewhat lackadaisical manner in which the passenger services were operated was probably attributable, at least in part, to the fact that they were almost certainly illegal. An essential requirement of railway life in Britain was that ALL lines which accommodated a revenue-earning passenger service had to be inspected by the Board of Trade, but there is no record of the BoT ever having inspected the C&HPR. The C&HPR and, after it, the LNWR, emphasised that passengers travelled on the line at their own risk and, furthermore, fares were not collected until the end of the journey - evidence, perhaps, that the railway companies were bending the rules by operating the service.

It has often been stated that the passenger services on the C&HPR ceased in 1876 or 1877, but there is photographic evidence to suggest that the 'fly' carriage - seemingly with passengers aboard - was still operating in the area in the mid-1890s. This might have been in connection with an unadvertised (unofficial?) passenger service between Buxton and Friden, which is thought to have operated from about 1892 to 1899. Unfortunately, as with so many other aspects of C&HPR history there is a conspicuous lack of substantiated information.

Goods Traffic

As already emphasised, the C&HPR was not a carrier, although it did own a small number of wagons which were sometimes made available. For most customers, though, the usual practice was for traffic to be conveyed either in private owner wagons or in contractors' wagons. In the early days, the maximum loads permitted were 6 tons for four-wheel wagons and 9 tons for six-wheel wagons - presumably, though, the six-wheel wagons were not taken up and down the inclines.

The C&HPR necessarily had certain criteria for private wagons used on the railway - for example, on 26 March 1833 a Mr.Needham of Tuncliffe was reminded that: *'....it is contrary to the present regulations to allow any waggon whatever to work upon the railway unless the wheels are three feet diameter and the soles case-hardened'.* On 7 December 1833 it was explained to Messrs. G. Wheatcroft that: *'The middle and drawing pieces of the framework of your waggons Nos.99 and 104 are too long to allow the preventors* (devices to hold the hauling cable centrally beneath the wagons) *to have sufficient clearance, and consequently are not safe when passing over the inclined planes .....by interlocking with abutting pieces of other waggons they frequently occasion damage....'* Wheatcroft's received another warning on 4 August 1834: *'.....there should be something fixed to the waggons to prevent the axles from cutting our tackling chains, several of which have nearly been sawn in two by them.....'*

From time to time, the C&HPR had to explain other facts of life to its customers - for example, on 6 May 1845 the railway company requested of Mr.A.H.Heathcote: *'You must be good enough to bear in mind that we cannot in future allow any more stones to pass along the railway or be lifted by the Crane, so excessively heavy as the last large one which you sent, which was 12 tons weight. I should be sorry not to afford you every accommodation in my power, but in attempting to deal with such weights as the one alluded to, we are running very great risk, and if persisted in will no doubt sooner or later cause a serious accident.'*

As for the traffic itself, when the C&HPR was conceived it was considered that the railway would help the development of local industries. The main local activity was quarrying - principally limestone - and probably the first major new quarry to open after the coming of the railway was at Grin (alternatively spelt Grinn), near Ladmanlow, on the north side of the Ladmanlow-Harpur Hill road. The quarry commenced operations in October 1832 - it appears that the C&HPR took advance orders for Grin stone, and for a short period before the quarry became operational the orders had to be fulfilled by increasing the output from Harpur Hill Quarry. Another quarry to open shortly after the coming of the railway was at Goyt's Moss, to the west of Burbage; it appears that the quarry was operational by 1834, but it seems not to have had a particularly productive or lengthy life.

In 1850 David Wheatcroft (that name again!) opened a quarry at Hopton Wood, on the west side of Middleton Moor. A half mile long steeply graded branch line was laid between the quarry and a point near the foot of Hopton Incline. It is unclear when the branch was laid - it is known to have been worked by a stationary engine, but a C&HPR directors' minute dated 28 August 1856 refers to the *proposed* stationary engine. That said, the possibility of the branch being open from the outset, and being worked by horses until 1856 or 1857, cannot be ruled out.

There was clearly a hiatus in operations at Hopton Wood Quarry in 1856/57 - almost certainly due to the contemporary economic climate - as the quarry is reported to have been closed during the whole of the second half-year period. It was still not operational well into 1857, although on 30 July the C&HPR's directors noted that: *'The Hopton and Middle Peak Quarries near Wirksworth have been taken, and are about to be extensively worked by a company formed for that purpose, and as the demand for that stone is only limited by the supply, the directors have found it necessary to incur some outlay in improving the line near Cromford to meet this additional traffic.'* Improvements were also planned for the Sheep Pasture-Middleton section itself, new rails being ordered in 1860.

The Middle Peak Quarry, referred to in the above report, was on the south side of the C&HPR - it was eventually served by a short branch line from a point near the foot of Middleton Incline. The quarry had been mentioned in the railway company's minutes in 1842, but operations had clearly ceased prior to 1856/57.

Also at Middleton, in 1857 William Wheatcroft started a quarry about half way down the incline. Earlier, on 28 November 1856, the C&HPR had agreed to: *'.....lay in sidings and points at his* (Wheatcroft's) *expense, on condition that he will guarantee a minimum tonnage of £150 in each year for seven years, and in addition to pay 2d per ton for haulage from the Cromford Plane to the Midland Railway....'* Later in 1857, the C&HPR's directors complained about *'.....Messrs W.Wheatcroft so working their quarries as to endanger breaking the rails and injuring the rope and generally to interfere with the traffic on the line.'*

While all this was taking place in the Middleton/Hopton Wood locality, about eighteen miles to the north-west the Buxton Line Company's operations at the Grin Quarries were prospering. At a meeting with the C&HPR directors on 12 October 1855, Mr Broom, on behalf of the Buxton Lime Co., stated that: *'.....it was the intention of*

the Company to increase the number of Kilns and consequently the amount of traffic on the line, provided the Railway Company will consent to reduce the rates of tonnage and haulage to an extent to enable the Buxton Lime Company to compete with the kilns at Dove Holes......' The C&HPR agreed to a whopping reduction from 10d to 6d per ton, effective when the kilns became operational, provided that there was a minimum payment of £1,000pa. The lime company, however, wanted an immediate reduction, and intimated that it wasn't altogether delighted with the service it had been receiving from the C&HPR, citing: 'irregularities in the conveyance of their lime to Whaley' and instances '.....of the lime being shaken off the waggons on the planes by the want of care of the engine men, and of a want of tarpaulins or cloths to keep the lime dry.'

The Buxton Lime Co. was well aware that it was one of the C&HPR's best customers, and played on this to secure a better deal which included a reduction in the proposed minimum annual payment from £1,000 to £700. The Buxton Co. also requested that the C&HPR construct and work a branch to the Grin lime kilns. The C&HPR was well aware that this would secure additional traffic, but it simply didn't have the funds available - it was estimated that the branch would cost £600, and there would be a similar sum on top for the wagons to handle the additional trade. The C&HPR's solution was to 'lend' (as it was termed) the lime company 1,600 yards of used rails so that the latter could lay the branch itself. The branch was opened early in 1857.

The next bout of railway development came in the 1880s, under LNWR auspices, when several sidings and short branch lines were laid to serve quarries. The longest new line of that period was the branch from Steeplehouse to Killer Bros. quarry at Middleton village. The quarry branch, which was laid in 1884, was some 1,200 yards long and had a ruling gradient of 1 in 27 - fortunately, though, it was downhill from the quarry (from a height of 820ft above sea level at the quarry to 717ft at Steeplehouse), and this obviously favoured the loads. The branch was worked by LNWR locomotives.

Services

In the early 1890s there was one train each way every weekday between Cromford Wharf and Whaley Bridge, and another each way between Cromford Wharf and Shallcross Bottom. A path was also available for an additional Cromford-Whaley Bridge train if required. Obviously, there were substantial alterations to the pattern of working following the changes of the 1890s, the Cromford-Parsley Hay and Hindlow-Ladmanlow sections effectively being regarded as separate entities, and much of the latter section being worked as a goods yard. As for passenger services during that period, from August 1899 there were two trains each way on weekdays between Buxton, Parsley Hay and Ashbourne, but a contemporary report opined that '....such a sparse level of service actually seems to be more than sufficient....'

Returning to the subject of goods traffic, by 1913 two mineral trains were scheduled each way between Cromford and Parsley Hay on weekdays, with an additional one from Cromford to Longcliffe on Saturdays. There were also two milk trains each day - one in the morning and one in the afternoon - from Longcliffe to Manchester. The balancing working was by means of a goods train (and milk empties) in the early morning from Pars-

On 12 July 1966 No.68012, one water tank and brake van cross Mouldridge Lane on the approach to Minninglow. At this time, it was far from unknown for the daily Middleton - Friden goods to comprise only a water tank or two - or sometimes only the brake van. The goods facilities at Minninglow had never been particularly extensive, but by 1966 they were all but non-existent. Note the photographer's famous Bentley, no doubt carefully posed! PHOTOGRAPH: IVO PETERS

ley Hay to Longcliffe. A morning milk train operated on Sundays - it left Longcliffe at 7.00am and reached Parsley Hay at 8.40am, from where it was taken on to Manchester. This was the only scheduled Sunday working on the line.

In the mid-1930s, there were two scheduled goods workings each weekday on the Middleton Top-Parsley Hay section. One of those trains, however, ran only as far as Friden, where it connected with a train from Buxton and then returned to Middleton. There was also the daily (Sundays included) milk trip from Longcliffe to Buxton (worked by a Buxton loco, which arrived with empties). At that time, there were two daily goods workings between Hindlow and Harpur Hill and two between Hindlow and Ladmanlow.

The milk trains from Longcliffe - a long-standing feature of C&HPR operations and the only regular Sunday working on the line - were discontinued during World War II and were not reinstated. By the mid-1950s the usual pattern was for one advertised working each way between Middleton Top and Friden, at which latter point it connected with a train to/from Buxton. There were also a handful of workings between Middleton Top and Hopton. The Sheep Pasture-Middleton and High Peak Junction-Cromford sections were worked 'as required'.

Rates

Surviving C&HPR documents make repeated references to the tolls charged for traffic, but the actual figures are somewhat misleading. As already emphasised, prior to the mid-1850s the C&HPR was *not* a carrier and so, for that period, the tolls quoted were merely for the right of passage - customers had to make their own arrangements for haulage, and if a contractor were required there was, obviously, an additional charge.

To give an idea of the charges of the period, in August 1832 the C&HPR quoted a potential customer 3/10^{1}/2d per ton (excluding haulage, of course) for stone conveyed the entire length of the railway (33 miles). The same customer also enquired about rates for conveying stone from Cromford Wharf to Manchester - via the railway to Whaley Bridge and thence via the Peak Forest Canal - and the C&HPR replied that one of their carriers, Messrs. G.Wheatcroft & Sons, who also had canal boats, would charge 14/- per ton for the whole journey.

A letter dated 26 April 1839 reveals that the C&HPR's current tolls (for the right of passage only) were calculated at 1^{1}/2d per ton per mile plus 1^{1}/2d per ton for each inclined plane, but traffic conveyed the entire length of the line was charged a reduced toll (still 3/10^{1}/2d per ton). Journeys of less than 12 miles were liable to an additional charge of 3d per ton, and traffic travelling less than 6 miles an additional 6d per ton. The usual rate for haulage at that time was ^{3}/4d per mile. Also in 1839, the C&HPR quoted 3/6^{1}/2d per ton (including the provision of wagons) for the transportation of iron ore from Haven Lodge (near Parsley Hay) to Whaley Bridge, a distance of some 20 miles. Another quote given in the same year was 3/6^{1}/2d per ton, inclusive of the provision of wagons, from Hurdlow Incline to Cromford, a distance of 17 miles.

By the late 1830s the lime and stone traffic conveyed over the C&HPR amounted to almost 30,000 tons annually, but although this was three times the quantity which had originally been estimated, it didn't automatically follow that the C&HPR was in splendid financial health. Far from it. Other traffic had fallen far short of expectation, but the C&HPR's main problem was that, almost from the outset, it had had to engage in a price war with rival canal companies - if the rivals

reduced their tolls, the C&HPR had to follow suit. This, of course, had the greatest effect on through traffic, which turned out to be nowhere near as abundant, and far less profitable, than had been anticipated. The bottom line was that the company was struggling.

Partly due to its poor financial position, the C&HPR was usually prepared to negotiate tolls for regular sources of traffic. For example, on 8 September 1842 the company agreed that : '....*the tonnage on coal taken for the purpose of burning lime to the Harpur Hill kilns belonging to Mr Gisbourn to be charged at 1/- per ton, and that the tonnage on lime from the same place be - over 22,000 tons per annum at 7d per mile, up to 17000 tons 8d, to 11000 tons 10d.'* In that instance, it might not have been irrelevant that the Mr.Gisbourn in question was also on the C&HPR's management committee. Indeed, several local businessmen and contractors were either on the board or the committee of the railway company, the Buxton Lime Co. being particularly well represented.

Although the C&HPR was not officially a carrier, the company often proved to be extremely flexible - possibly because it had to bend over backwards to attract and secure whatever traffic was available. One example of the company's eagerness to help is evidenced in a letter from John Leonard (the C&HPR's general manager) to Messrs. John Shaw, timber merchants of Manchester on 10 May 1845. Leonard explained that the toll for timber 'going through' was 2/8d per ton, '....but we are charging other parties 5/6 per ton; in this case we find waggons and haulage but the charge does not include loading'. However, Leonard had to admit that, at that time, the C&HPR didn't actually have any spare wagons.

The timber company's subsequent action can be gauged from a letter from John Leonard dated 1 July (1845): *'I have been informed that since you spoke to me respecting waggons for the conveyance of your timber you have made another arrangement with Messrs. Wheatcrofts and have agreed with them for the carriage of it. To this I have no objection whatever as we are so extremely short of waggons that it is impossible for us to accommodate everyone; I think, however, that after such treatment you can hardly expect that we shall at all times have waggons for you whenever it may suit your convenience to ask for or use them. I am desirous at all times to accommodate everyone as far as we have the means, but I cannot permit the company to be made fools of.'* So there!

The C&HPR wasn't always prepared to tug its corporate forelock. In July 1849 the company received an enquiry from the Butterley Iron Works, near Alfreton, about conveying 700 tons of bridge work destined for Liverpool. The Butterley Co. requested a reduced rate from the C&HPR otherwise they would send the cargoes via the Grand Trunk Canal to Runcorn. After procrastinating for three months the C&HPR's blunt reply to the Butterley Co. was that: *'.....in the absence of any information being supplied by you to justify the reduction the directors are at a loss to know on what ground you apply for a reduction.'* Conspicuously, there is no further correspondence on that subject.

Among the many references to tolls and rates, we find that on 23 January 1851: *'.....Messrs Cawley and Heginbotham, barytes manufacturers, have agreed to pay 4d per ton on coal and 6d per ton on barytes between the bottom of Shallcross Inclined plane and Whaley Bridge.'* (The barytes were apparently destined for Hull). A letter to Thomas Carstairs on 30 April 1851 quoted: *'.....tonnage on coal from Cromford to Ladmanlow 2/5d per ton; from Whaley to Ladmanlow 1/2d per ton. Rates include wharf dues.'* Hauling was still quoted as $^3/_4$d per ton per mile and the use of waggons at $^1/_4$d per ton per mile. On 4 September 1851 we find that: *'.....slate from Whaley to Parsley Hay and Longcliff reduced to 2/- per ton .....manure from Parsley Hay and Longcliff to Steeple House reduced to 6d per ton for the whole distance.'*

By the mid-1850s the limestone traffic was considered to be 'increasing steadily', and the tolls for coal from Cromford to Ladmanlow (for burning the lime) were reduced from 2/3d to 1/6d per ton.

Railway and Carrier

One aspect of the C&HPR's reconstitution in 1855 was that the company could act as carriers, and on 27 February 1856 the committee presented to the directors an inventory of rolling stock:

Common waggons without springs used for coal etc.	82
Harper (sic) *Hill lime wagons*	45
Goods spring waggons	14
Coal Spring Waggons for Whaley	4
Trucks	2
Under repairs	7
New Sample Truck	1
Passenger Carriage	1
TOTAL	**156**

Plus eight canal boats for coal and one for goods. Plus twenty horses.

As already mentioned, in its 'non-carrier' days the C&HPR owned a number of waggons, but no precise details are known as to types, number etc. Given the quantity of 'common' waggons noted in the above inventory, it is possible that some of those

had been inherited, in some manner or another, from private traders or contractors. Whatever the origins of the wagons, the committee considered that '.....the above stock affords the means not only of fully carrying on the present amount of traffic, but also of meeting an increased trade, particularly in general merchandise, which is one of the most remunerative branches of the business'.

The directors shared the optimism, noting, at that same meeting, that: *'The coal traffic is an important source of revenue and pays well, as the full rates of Tonnage are charged and there is also a profit on the sale of coal carried on the Railway. The quantity last year exceeded £13,000 tons, producing a gross tonnage of about £1,300 exclusive of the profits derived from the sale'.* Another encouraging note concerned a proposed warehouse at Whaley Bridge and the recapture of the flour trade (mentioned in Chapter One). It was also noted that although the Hopton Stone Quarry had been closed during the whole of the previous half-year (in the corresponding period in 1854 they had generated £224 worth of trade), the quarries had recently been re-let and traffic would hopefully be restored.

The corporate optimism was not wholly unjustified, as the following year - on 30 July 1857 - the directors reported: *'.....an increase in revenue during the last half year of £148.18.3 arising principally from Minerals',* and in February 1858: *'....a half-year improvement of £190.1.4d, despite the adverse state of commercial affairs which has peculiarly affected the minerals trade'.* However, the improvement, although very welcome, was still not sufficient to pay the current interest. The C&HPR had to continue its eternal struggle.....

Water

On the limestone hills traversed by the C&HPR, water was sometimes a sought after commodity, not only for railway purposes, but also for local residents. It was therefore necessary for it to be transported, in tanks, to various points along the line, and the railway continued to serve this important function until the very end of its existence.

Reverting briefly to the railway's formative years, the problem of an adequate water supply for the stationary engines had been appreci-

ated at a very early stage, and solutions were still being sought after the railway had opened. On 14 July 1834 the C&HPR's general manager and engineer, John Leonard, reported on: *'.....the work we have been doing at Middleton Moor for the purpose of procuring water for the engines.....'* , explaining that: *'.....the entrance to the heading being left open, some mischievous people had been in and caused an accumulation of rubbish which had obstructed the passage of the water. I directed that it be cleaned out and that a door be placed at the entrance....'* This was rather embarrassing for John Leonard and the C&HPR, as neither had obtained permission to tap the source in the first place, let alone enclose it. It seems, however, that matters were satisfactorily resolved.

For much of the C&HPR's long existence, the passage of water tanks was a very familiar sight. The tanks were converted locomotive tenders, some of which dated back to the 1850s, having been built at Wolverton Works during the superintendency of John McConnell. Some of the tenders were four-wheeled while others had started life as six-wheelers, but in the case of the latter type the middle wheels had been removed so that they could be taken up and down the inclines on the C&HPR. Most of the water tanks were filled at Cromford Goods, the supply being a spring in the hillside above the railway, but full tanks were also brought in from Buxton.

During the BR era there were 21 water tanks in regular use on the C&HPR, and an average of about 100 tank-loads were dispatched from Cromford each month. The water supplied the winding engines and locomotive sheds at Sheep Pasture and Middleton, and was also used for locomotive purposes at Longcliffe, a row of tanks being kept on a raised siding for that purpose. (A similar raised water tank siding had once existed near Dowlow). Water tanks were also stationed at Hopton Top, Parsley Hay and Hurdlow, but these were for domestic purposes - indeed, the occupants of several remote cottages and farmhouses at those points had to rely exclusively on the mobile tanks for their water supplies. Latterly, the water tanks were also used to supply 1,000 gallons per day, under contract, to the Prestwich & Sons Intake Quarry near Middleton.

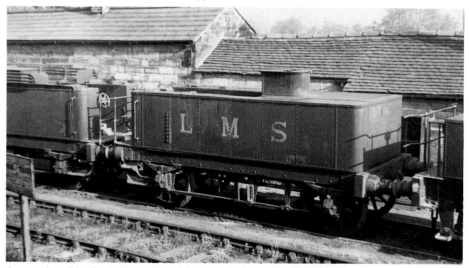

As mentioned in the text, converted loco tenders were used as mobile water tanks and were positioned at various key locations along the C&HPR. Most of the tenders dated back to the Webb, Ramsbottom or even McConnell eras and, if necessary, had been converted to four-wheelers so that they could be taken up and down the inclines. This picture was taken at Cromford in 1952 (ignore the 'LMS' lettering!), the rake of tenders having been brought down the incline from Sheep Pasture. PHOTOGRAPH: DEREK CLAYTON

5....And finally....

Due to an act of vandalism, on 30 July 1955 0-4-0ST No.47000 derailed and overturned at Steeplehouse, coming to rest in the garden of Station House. The rerailing operation took place on 1 August, a makeshift track being laid on a bed of sleepers for the purpose. PHOTOGRAPH: E.R.MORTEN

At the time of Nationalisation in 1948 the C&HPR line was doing reasonably steady business - steady enough, in fact, for BR to consider various improvements. Some improvements were indeed made but there was another side to the proverbial coin as, in April 1952, the northern extremity of the line - Whaley Bridge to the Canal Wharves, including Whaley Bridge Incline (horse worked to the end) - was closed. Nevertheless, the short section between Whaley Bridge station and Shallcross Yard remained open, and continued to be used by BR until January 1965.

On 4 August 1954, following a decline in traffic in the Ladmanlow area, the section of line between Ladmanlow and Old Harpur closed, thereby truncating the C&HPR at the latter point. That same year - on 1 November - passenger services were withdrawn from the Buxton-Ashbourne line, thus reducing Hindlow, Dowlow and Parsley Hay stations to the status of goods only. Hurdlow station, on that same section, had closed to all traffic as from 15 August 1949.

In the mid-1950s one train each weekday was adequate for the traffic from Middleton Top to Friden - the usual departure time was 9.05am from Middleton. At Friden, a 3F 0-6-0 would take over from the C&HPR loco - the 3F arrived at 9.40am with empties from Buxton and departed at 12.30pm (SO) or 1.55pm (SX) for Hindlow, where it would collect wagons ex-Old Harpur before returning to Buxton. During the same period, High Peak Junction was served by two 'main line' trains each weekday. One arrived from Derby (St.Marys) at 10.30am and left for home at 12.40pm, the other arriving at 12.55pm from Rowsley and departing for Chaddesden at 2.15pm.

Still in the mid-1950s, on 30 July 1955 there was an accident at Steeplehouse Goods. Vandals had altered the points, and 0-4-0ST No.47000 derailed, careered down a slope, and came to rest in the garden of Station House. As there were no injuries, and as members of the public had not been involved, a Ministry of Transport enquiry was not necessary. There was, however, an internal enquiry, prompted by the allegation that the engine had been left unattended with the brake not screwed down. No.47000 was rerailed on 1 August, and after repair it returned to work on the High Peak line, finishing its days in October 1966 at Rowsley shed.

By the late 1950s the usual working practice on weekdays on the Middleton Top-Parsley Hay section was for the early morning train to Friden to be double headed (by J94s) as far as Hopton Top. At that point the pilot engine was detached, and continued its day with shunting duties at the various quarries on that section. The remainder of the train carried on to Friden, dropping and picking up wagons *en route* at Hopton Top, Harborough Brick Works and Longcliffe. At Friden, the locomotive from Buxton took over, and the J94 returned to Middleton, dropping and picking up wagons as necessary. On Saturdays the procedure was slightly different, the C&HPR train from Middleton Top working through to Parsley Hay to meet a Buxton-Ashbourne goods, which was usually in the charge of an ex-LNWR 0-8-0.

On the Old Harpur section of the line, in the late 1950s there were usually three workings each way on weekdays:

8.00am ex-Briggs Siding, arr.Old Harpur 9.20am; dep.Old Harpur 10.15am, arr.Buxton 12.28pm.

3.15pm ex-Buxton, arr.Harpur Hill 4.05pm; dep.Harpur Hill 5.20pm, arr.Buxton 7.25pm.

6.00pm ex-Hindlow, arr.Harpur Hill 6.10pm; dep.Harpur Hill 6.20pm, arr.Hindlow 6.25pm.

As discussed elsewhere in this booklet, by the end of 1960 the J94s were in total control of the Middleton Top-Friden section, but beyond Friden a change was seen in May 1962 when LMR 2-6-0 No.46429 went on loan from Stoke to Buxton for use on the Buxton-Friden goods. Until then, the Buxton working over the C&HPR between Parsley Hay and Friden had been the only remaining one at Buxton exclusively diagrammed for a 3F 0-6-0, the most regular engine on that duty having been No.43278.

WEEKDAYS			PARSLEY HAY AND MIDDLETON						
DOWN		J	J	J	J	J	J	J
			8.15 am Empties from Buxton	7.55 am from Buxton		1.35 am from Hopton Quarry		
		74		74	75	74		75
Mileage M C			FX	FO				
0 0 PARSLEY HAY arr			am	am	am	PM	am	PM
dep			8 53	8 55				
2 26 Friden arr			9 25	9 25				
dep			9 40	9 40				
7 63 Longcliffe arr dep					11 55			
10 16 Hopton (Top) arr		8 15			12 25	1 45		
dep				12 0	1 10	1 50	2 40	
11 0 Hopton Quarry arr		8 20			1 23			
dep		8 30			2 0			
11 31 MIDDLETON (TOP) arr		8 40		12 5	2 5	1 58	2 45	

UP		J	J	J	J	J	J	J
				To Hindlow		To Hindlow		To Hindlow
		74	75	74	74	74	75	
Mileage M C			SO	SX				
0 0 MIDDLETON (TOP) dep		am	am	PM	PM	PM	PM	2 30
		7 35	9 5	11 15	12 30	12 40		
0 23 Hopton Quarry arr		7 45						
1 15 Hopton (Top) arr		8 5	9 15	11 20		1 35	1 45	2 35
dep		8V10	9 35			1 50		
1 77 Harbor'o Sdgs arr dep			9 40 9 55					
7 48 Longcliffe arr dep			9 55 11 35					
9 5 Friden arr dep					12 30		1 55	
11 31 PARSLEY HAY arr					12 45		2 13	

LMR Working Timetable, 17 June 1957 until further notice.

On 3 June 1963 Middleton Incline was closed, thereby bisecting the C&HPR. Closure, as mentioned earlier, was principally due to the poor condition of the engine house boiler - installed in 1959 and already, even by then, an ancient part of a Ramsbottom 0-6-0. Repair had not been considered worthwhile as most of the traffic on the Middleton section was taken via Sheep Pasture Incline - though the Middleton section actually generated a useful amount of traffic.

On the Middleton Top-Friden/Parsley Hay section, the branch to Hopton Wood Stone Quarries closed in June 1962 after some 110 years of operation. Fortunately, there was another source of regular traffic on that section - the Prestwich & Sons Intake Quarry, which actually became the main source of traffic between Middleton and Friden during the C&HPR's last few years. Traffic could be quite heavy at times; for example, a visitor to the line on 1 September 1965 noted that the morning train to Friden, hauled by J94 No.68012, comprised ten wagons of ballast (from the Prestwich quarry), two water tanks and a brake van. That load necessitated four trips up Hopton Incline. Frustratingly for the BR, the loading gauge on the Middleton Top-Parsley Hay section was very tight, and so the largest wagons which could be used were 16-ton minerals and a few relatively uncommon types. Such wagons were not only virtually obsolete, but also, in terms of carrying capacity, uneconomic.

Although the traffic from Prestwich Quarry could sometimes be quite heavy, that was not always the case. Indeed, it was far from unknown for the daily Middleton-Friden trains to comprise nothing more than a couple of water tanks. The erratic flow of traffic, combined with the inability to use large mineral wagons, the limited options for motive power (the J94s weren't going to be around for ever, and 350hp diesels had previously proved to be unsuitable), the very nature of the line (still with an inclined plane at its southern end), and the contemporary ethos of 'if it doesn't make a profit, cut it', had only one consequence - closure.

Closure of the C&HPR did not actually take place all at once. In the four years following the closure of Middleton Incline in 1963, sections were closed in a piecemeal manner - for the sake of clarity the pertinent dates are listed below. The last parts of the 'real' C&HPR were dispensed with in 1967. The Middleton Top-Friden section officially closed to public traffic as from Monday 1 May, and the Friden-Parsley Hay-Briggs Siding section as from 2 October. This left the Briggs Siding-Harpur Hill section still open, but that portion had been realigned and upgraded to such an extent that it could hardly be regarded as 'proper' C&HPR. For the record, though, regular traffic between Harpur Hill and Hindlow ceased in January 1973 and that section was officially closed in September. This left only a short and much altered stretch of 'C&HPR' near Dowlow (a continuation of the line from Buxton), which actually remains open to this day, serving the ICI kilns. Today, limestone is brought in from Tunstead (on the Peak Forest line) to fire the limeburning kilns - something of a reversal of how things used to be!

Summary of closure dates - BR period
10.4.52: Whaley Bridge Incline and Wharf
2.8.1954: Old Harpur-Ladmanlow
1.11.54: *Passenger services withdrawn*, Buxton-Parsley Hay-Ashbourne
21.6.59: *Line singled*, Parsley Hay-Briggs Siding
12.6.62: Hopton Wood Quarry branch
3.6.63: Middleton Incline
2.3.64: Middle Peak branch (Steeplehouse)
6.7.64: *Redesignation*, Friden reclassified as a coal depot
30.1.65: Shallcross Yard-Whaley Bridge station
2.2.66: Old Harpur-Harpur Hill
3.4.67: High Peak Jctn-Sheep Pasture-Middleton Foot

1.5.67: Middleton Top-Friden
2.10.67: Friden-Parsley Hay
29.10.67: High Peak Junction signal box
21.11.67: Parsley Hay-Briggs Siding
19.9.73: Harpur Hill-Hindlow

Railtours
Inevitably, a railway as distinctive as the C&HPR was a popular venue for railtours. Some of the tours of the 1950s and 1960s are listed below - it does not pretend to be exhaustive.

25 April 1953: Joint SLS/Manchester Locomotive Society railtour. North London tanks Nos.58856 and 58860 were used to haul a fully-fitted train of four open trucks and three brake vans from Middleton Top to Friden. At Friden, 3F 0-6-0 No.43618 plus three corridor coaches took over and conveyed the party to Ladmanlow, and thence back to Hindlow and Buxton.

27 June 1953: A repeat of the above, by popular demand.

21 May 1955: Gloucestershire Railway Society railtour. Two of the ever popular North London tanks, Nos.58850 and 58856, worked a train of four opens and a brake van from Parsley Hay to Middleton Top.

25 September 1955: Nos.58850 and 58860 worked a special between Middleton Top and Friden. Details unknown.

3 May 1959: Special working from Friden to Middleton Top, hauled by North London tank No.58850.

30 September 1961: J94 No.68006 on a special. Details unknown.

27 June 1964: RCTS railtour, originating at Sheffield. The C&HPR portion commenced at Parsley Hay, where J94s Nos.68012 and 68079, described as 'grimy', hauled a train of six opens and five brakes to Middleton Top. From Middleton Foot to Sheep Pasture Top the party was conveyed in open wagons hauled by 0-4-0ST No.47006, and from Cromford to High Peak Junction by J94 No.68006.

29 August 1964: J94s Nos.68012 and 68079 worked a special. Details unknown.

30 April 1967: There were three 'Last Day' tours, all double headed by J94s Nos.68006 and 68012. On the first trip, with six brake vans, the locomotives stalled half way up Hopton Incline and had to return to the foot and make two separate trips with three vans. The second special of the day was even more inauspicious, the two locomotives stalling on Hopton Incline with only four brake vans in tow. Again, the train had to be divided before a successful ascent could be made. On the third trip - which was also the final empty working through to Buxton - the train, comprising four brake vans, completed the journey at the first attempt. Great Days!

Heading for the hills............ PHOTOGRAPH: DEREK CLAYTON